Possessed
Possessions 2

More
Haunted antiques, furniture
and collectibles

Possessed Possessions 2
More Haunted Antiques, Furniture and Collectibles
First Edition

Copyright 1998 by Edward M. Okonowicz Jr.
All rights reserved.

ISBN   1-890690-02-3

Published by
Myst and Lace Publishers, Inc.
1386 Fair Hill Lane
Elkton, Maryland 21921

Printed in the U.S.A.
by Victor Graphics

Photography, Typography and Design
by Kathleen Okonowicz

Dedications

To Bruce Henrickson, Al and Olga Manners, Jerry Maisel,
Bernie Dworsky, Elbert Chance, Al Roberson and Mary Hempel
Ed Okonowicz

To my grandsons,
Arthur, Jacob and Tyler
Kathleen Burgoon Okonowicz

Acknowledgments

The author and illustrator appreciate the assistance of those
who have played an important role in this project.

Special thanks are extended to
the following friends for their assistance

including

John Brennan
Barbara Burgoon
Sue Moncure
Connie Okonowicz
Marianna Preston
Ted Stegura
and
Monica Witkowski
for their proofreading and suggestions;

and, of course,

particular appreciation to the hosts of the antique ghosts.

Also available from
Myst and Lace Publishers, Inc.

Spirits Between the Bays Series

Volume I
Pulling Back the Curtain
(October, 1994)

Volume IV
In the Vestibule
(August, 1996)

Volume II
Opening the Door
(March, 1995)

Volume V
Presence in the Parlor
(April, 1997)

Volume III
Welcome Inn
(September, 1995)

Volume VI
Crying in the Kitchen
(April, 1998)

Stairway over the Brandywine
A Love Story
(February, 1995)

Possessed Possessions
Haunted Antiques, Furniture and Collectibles
(March, 1996)

Possessed Possessions 2
More Haunted Antiques, Furniture and Collectibles
(August 1998)

Disappearing Delmarva
Portraits of the Peninsula People
(August, 1997)

FIRED!
A DelMarVa Murder Mystery
(May, 1998)

Table of Contents

All of the stories are the result of interviews with those who experienced the events. In some cases, written materials—in the form of letters, articles and newspaper clippings—were provided. In most of these stories the real names of the participants have been changed.

*The actual names are used only in these chapters.

Introduction

*S*ince the release of *Possessed Possessions: Haunted Antiques, Furniture and Collectibles* in the spring of 1996, we have received reports of more unusual events associated with items that logically should not have a spirit of their own. Many of the fascinating stories that have resulted from these leads are included in this book.

The strange events that we've discovered range from the humorous, involving the pesky piano and the talking candlestick; to the fascinating, concerning the Ash Lady's dresser, a confused cupboard, agitated ambrotypes and talking vegetables; to the horrifying, such as a mysterious mirror, the cursed crib, a demonic bed and a bizarre collection of wicked woodcarvings.

Unfortunately, there were more leads and suggestions than we were able to include in this book, the final issue of our two-volume *Possessed Possessions* series. However, additional stories associated with haunted objects will be included in each of the remaining books to be issued in our 13-volume "Spirits Between the Bays" ghost/folklore series.

Beginning with Vol. VII, *Up the Back Stairway*, we will include tales of diabolical dolls, agitated antiques, phantom paintings and creepy collectibles.

Throughout our search, we discovered that many of those who have experienced unusual events associated with bothersome objects proclaim that they will never buy a used item again. But, on one occasion a collector stated that she is very willing to give interesting pieces a chance.

I met this lady in a small antique shop, and she told me, "I don't buy anything new. I only buy second hand stuff because it has personality. If it's friendly, I keep it. If not, I get rid of it. If you enjoy experiencing spirits and talking to them as I do, it's an adventure. And if it doesn't work out, I just get rid of it."

Those not in the market for haunted objects may read our new collection of stories featuring interesting items that have called out for attention and captured the fancy of others. Some of the owners have had good experiences and an equal number have not.

Many have gotten rid of their finds, but a few, even though they admit they are afraid, continue to keep their possessions—and in some cases they can't explain why.

In closing, here is a final note of advice: "If the cost of an antique—or any other item, including a home—seems too good to be true, there's a very good chance that it is possessed."

Happy Haunted Hunting.

—Ed Okonowicz
in Fair Hill, Maryland,
at the northern edge of
the Delmarva Peninsula
—Fall 1998

Domestic Disturbance

*M*ark was waiting for me at the diner on Route 40, two miles east of the Baltimore city limits. It was a perfect place to meet a big city cop: stainless steel siding, neon signs, Formica tables and a jukebox playing oldies.

The coffee cups were plain, with thin gold and brown lines circling the top edge, just like you'd expect in a vintage, open-'round-the-clock greasy spoon. Mark wasn't a surprise either. You could pick him out from among the small number of patrons who were still there at midnight.

He was a big man, about 6 feet 2 inches tall, with a heavy frame that filled the booth to the right of the cashier. He had been a Baltimore policeman for 10 years.

Looking at him, it would be hard to imagine a situation where he would be smaller than the person he was pursuing.

We had arranged the meeting at the end of his shift. With court appearances, unexpected overtime, staggered shift work and limited windows of opportunity for definite time off, it was hard to get a time when we both could get together.

We grabbed what we could, and this was it.

Besides, the topic of our conversation was one that Mark didn't want to talk about in the district headquarters or at home.

Our subject was ghosts, or the unexplained.

Either way, Mark stressed, both on the phone and in person, they were not subjects that he believed in or even cared about. But, he had told me over the phone, what happened did happen, and after several years he still didn't have any logical explanation.

After brief introductions and greetings, he ordered me a coffee. The waitress came and went, and we got down to the nitty gritty.

"Look," he began, "I've been a cop for a good while, and I've had more than my share of unusual incidents that often seemed to start out well but turn out bad. But there was nothing ever like this."

According to Mark, the word both in and beyond district headquarters was: If something strange was going to happen, Mark would be involved in some way.

Eventually, Mark learned to relish his role as the station oddball, and he became a loner, never attending any parties or outside office events. While on duty he rarely talked, did his job, filed his reports and went home without as much as saying good night.

But silence and dedication to duty did not break the spell associated with his ability to attract weird cases, the most bizarre occurring on a hot August night when he would rather have been home, watching the Orioles, with the AC blasting and having a cold one from the fridge.

> **❝**I've been a cop for a good while, and I've had more than my share of unusual incidents that often seemed to start out well but turn out bad. But there was nothing ever like this.**❞**

"Me and this new kid, Ralph or Rick, I don't remember his name now. But it doesn't matter, he's not on the force anymore. We got a call to go to Liberty Heights. I'll never forget that night. It happened in an old house, three stories high, standing at the end of the block."

As they started to approach the front door, Mark said they heard noise, like furniture being thrown around, upstairs.

"We figured there was a riot going on up in there," Mark said, "and were ready to fly through the door and charge up the stairs. But this small lady, who opened the front door, led us into the living room, just to the right of the entrance hallway.

"The whole family—the father, mother and three kids—are all huddled together, on the couch in the living room, and they look like they're scared to death."

Mark recalled that the father walked over to him and said the noise had started suddenly, about an hour earlier. The whole family ran downstairs, and he called the police. They thought some kids had broken a window, gotten in from the fire escape on the second floor and were destroying the house.

Mark and Rick told the family to shut the living room door and wait for them to return.

Slowly, the two officers ascended the stairs toward the second floor.

"Now, before I go on," Mark said, "I want to tell you that I don't believe in this supernatural stuff. Never did, anyway. But as we moved up the steps, we both heard banging and it sounded like a gang was up there smashing up the place."

But as soon as Mark, who was in the lead, stepped on the second-floor hall landing, the noise stopped—suddenly and totally. "It was as if it just disappeared," Mark said, sipping his coffee and shaking his head.

He said both he and Rick checked every room together, looked in the closets, shined their flashlights under the beds.

"We even pulled back the shower curtain and then made sure all the windows were locked and secure. I tell you, nobody and nothing was up there."

As they started to return downstairs, the noise started up again. This time it was coming from the third floor, and it was just as loud as before.

"We looked at each other, drew our weapons," said Mark, "and I nodded in the direction of the stairs to the third floor. We went up, slowly, approaching the latest noise that was going full force.

"I swear, I was sure we were going to find at least three or four guys up there tearing hell outta the place. And just like before, as soon as I put my foot on the third floor hallway, the noise stopped, totally."

Mark and Rick checked every room, even though most were empty of furniture. All the windows were locked. Again, nothing was found in any of the closets or rooms.

"Thinking back now," Mark said, "I remember thinking one thing was really strange. In the largest, practically empty room, there was this single chair. It had curved arms, a bright red seat and a lot of carving on the back, like birds' or angels' wings. It was sitting by itself, all alone, way off in a corner. It was really far away from the door.

"When I looked in that room, it just seemed odd, almost as if the chair was staring at me. I remember thinking that exact thought at the time, then I laughed to myself and put it out of my mind and shut the door, slamming it tight and hearing the latch catch."

Not finding or hearing anything else, Mark began descending the steps to the second floor and Rick fell in behind. They had holstered their weapons and neither was talking. Mark said they were listening in case the disturbance started up again.

When they got to the second floor landing it was still completely quiet.

"When we get halfway down the steps, between the second and first floor," Mark said, "we hear this sound, like something is falling over itself and heading down, in our direction. It was getting louder, sounding sort of like a person was falling down the steps. But it wasn't a person hitting the steps, it was more like wood crashing against wood. And it was getting closer.

"We looked up and couldn't see anything," Mark said. Then he paused, looked across the booth of the diner and whispered to me, "I tell ya, I was scared by now and rather than go up, I told Rick we're going down. So I continued walking toward the first floor.

"The next thing I knew, Rick was falling on top of my back and knocking me down. And I'm face down and flat on my chest and something is flying over my body, heading down, for the main floor hallway."

When Mark and Rick pulled themselves up, the chair, the solitary chair that Mark had seen in the large room on the third floor, was sitting, facing him at the foot of the stairs.

"I know this may sound crazy now," Mark said, "but we both drew our weapons and slowly headed toward the chair. I was going to blast the hell outta it if it moved again.

"I yelled for the family to stay inside and not come out, and they didn't." Mark let out a short laugh. "I didn't have to tell them twice to stay put."

The two officers grabbed the chair, lifted it up, looked underneath and moved it around. There was no explanation for what had occurred.

"We tied the chair to the banister with clothes line," said Mark, "and we went upstairs and checked the whole building again.

"There were no drop ceilings where someone could hide, no way anyone could have gotten in and fooled us. It was just us and the chair.

"But I remember shutting the third floor door tightly," Mark said. "That chair couldn't get out on its own. Someone, something or some force had to help it get loose."

Mark and Rick agreed not to call for a backup unit. They wrote up the report as a domestic disturbance that had been settled, therefore, no arrest would have been necessary.

"We told the family that we were getting out of there and that they should, too," Mark said. "In fact, we drove them to a relative's house to spend the night. I went back once to check on them. It was a few months later, but they had moved out and there was another family living there."

Mark paused.

"I was tempted to ask the new people about anything strange that they may have seen or experienced," said Mark, "but they didn't volunteer anything when I was there, so I let it go. I did peek inside, just in case I saw the chair there, but didn't see anything familiar. It was gone. I guess it probably walked off on its own one night."

Mark took a final sip of coffee, said nothing else, and went for his wallet to leave a tip.

I waited, letting him decide what he wanted to say next.

"You can believe it or not," he added. "That's the way it was and it won't change. I don't know how, or why, or even why it was me there that night. Just luck of the draw, I guess.

"I gave up figuring it out a long time ago."

Then, standing up to leave, Mark looked down and said, "Go ahead and use it, the story in your book. Maybe you or somebody else can come up with some kind of answer that will make some sense. If you ever do, give me a call."

I haven't been able to come up with a reason to recontact Mark, not yet anyway.

Cursed Crib

Rachel is part Cherokee Indian. Her ancestors lived in the mountains of North Carolina and, growing up, her grandmother taught her about the earthly things—like folk medication, faith healing, signs in the woods, power of the medicine woman and the wisdom of elders.

"When you learn that when you're young, it stays with you," she said. "It's embedded in you. You don't laugh about it. Everything that happens means something. No matter where I go or live, what I learned will never leave me. All of it will be with me day and night. It's just a fact of life."

Today, Rachel lives in downstate Delaware, below the canal, on a main road leading to the beaches. She used to live up near Newark, not far from the Chrysler auto plant, where her first husband worked on the assembly line.

Their house was a basic split level—bedrooms on the top floor, living room and kitchen looking out on the lawn and a recreation room downstairs, beside the utility room and small, half basement.

The events happened in 1970, nearly 30 years ago, when Rachel was in her mid 20s, when she was pregnant with her daughter Christine.

"My husband liked old things, and so did I," she recalled. "One day, he came home with a cast iron crib—the kind with spirals and lots of design. It was painted white, and it looked real cute and sort of Victorian. He said some woman he worked with wanted to get rid of it, so he bought it."

Rachel prepared a room for the new baby next to the master bedroom. After she returned with her daughter from the hospital, she placed little Christine in the Victorian crib in the freshly painted bedroom.

"That very first night," Rachel recalled, "I started having nightmares. They were so real that I had to get up and go next door and check on the baby. I had this dream that there was something hovering over the crib, a heavy, dark cloud, and that it was going to suffocate my baby.

"As the dream continued, I tried to get to Christine, but something was stopping me. So I couldn't get there to save her. I would wake up crying and sweating and have to go to check, to see if she was still breathing.

"I was so scared to go in there," Rachel added, "that I remember creeping down the hall with my eyes closed. Then, I would reach my hand in a crack in the door and turn the light on before I dared go into the room. I was so afraid of what was in there. But, I would see my daughter was okay and felt better. Sometimes, I would sit beside her all night until morning. Other times, I would go back into my own bed."

As expected, this was upsetting Rachel's husband, who told her she was crazy and causing him to lose sleep.

Eventually, the feeling of fear associated with the middle of the night dreams began to occur during the day.

"All day long," Rachel recalled, "I'd be worried. I'd be in the living room and I'd have to run upstairs and check on my baby. I was going crazy. I was worried during the day and staying up from the nightmares all night. I was a basket case. My nerves were shot."

Eventually, Rachel shared her problem with a friend, who immediately suggested the problem might be the ornate antique crib. Since there was no other explanation, Rachel agreed to hold a yard sale and get rid of the crib. "Surely," her friend said, "someone would buy the attractive wrought iron antique."

On the morning of the bargain sale, the crib sold within 20 minutes. In fact, Rachel had gone into the house for a few moments. When she came back out, it was gone. She never knew who the new owner was.

But, she recalled, all her tension seemed to leave when the crib was sold.

"I didn't have any fear anymore," Rachel said. "It was all gone. Now, it may not mean much to you, but I was going through hell every single day and night for more than three months. Just hearing about it, you can't understand the fear and how it changed my mood and disposition. Plus, my husband was shouting at me all the time about how nuts I was, and he couldn't get his rest. It was a real mess.

"But, the minute I took the Victorian crib down, all the fear was gone. I was so relieved. The other crib was just a plain, wooden cheapie, but with no problems. I will admit that it took a while to get the heebie jeebies out of my system."

A few months later, at a United Auto Workers family picnic, Rachel's husband pointed to a group of people eating at a nearby picnic table. At the far end was the woman from whom he had bought the Victorian crib.

"I immediately wanted to go over and talk to her," Rachel said. "Really, I wanted to see if I could find out anything about the crib. When I got a chance to get to her, I introduced myself as the lady who had her crib. I told her I recently sold it and wanted to talk to her for a few minutes. But, she acted stiff and cold, like she didn't want to talk to me about it at all."

Rachel walked away and was both hurt and embarrassed. She decided that the woman was probably upset because she hadn't given her the first opportunity to buy the crib back. Apparently, it was a collector's item and the lady was upset that it had gone to a stranger.

Later, however, Rachel ran into the lady again and immediately apologized for not returning the crib.

"She stared at me," Rachel recalled, "and she said, real serious like, 'I never want to see that crib again.' And then she told me why."

The lady said she had lived in a trailer park in Elkton, Maryland. One day, she left her baby asleep in the Victorian crib while she went next door to get her hair done.

"While at her neighbor's," Rachel said, "her trailer caught on fire. It was one of those old trailers that was filled with stuff that burned real fast. The fire started in the back. The baby was in the front. They heard people screaming outside and smelled smoke. When they got there, they dragged the baby and the crib outside the front door.

"The baby didn't have any burns on it, and the crib was untouched too. Not burned at all. It was the smoke, filled with chemicals and fumes that killed her baby. He was suffocated from the black smoke.

"I was shaking as I heard what happened. I felt so bad for her, and I couldn't tell her what happened to me. She felt so guilty, that she went next door and her baby died. There was no consoling her. It was her fault. It would be her fault until the day she died."

Naturally, Rachel thought about the dreams, her fears, what had happened to her while she had the crib.

"Most people may think that the black cloud was coming after my baby. But, I don't believe that. I think that the dead baby's spirit was with me, warning me. It was still there, hanging around that crib. You see, my baby had a severe breathing problem. So it was warning me to keep a close eye on my baby. Who knows what might have happened if I didn't look in on her as much as I did. That's what I think about the whole thing. As a result of it all, I kept an eye on my daughter more than normal.

"But, I never want to go through something like that again. The cold sweat, teary eyes, heavy breathing, being scared all the time. After a while, I was so afraid, I didn't want to go down the hall and get near that room. I'd have to force myself to take one step at a time. I was a mother and it was my child. After I turned the light on, I'd walk around the room several times, to make

> **"**I never saw anything. I just dreamed it all, but there was a presence, and it was in that room. It stayed after I turned the light on, and it was up there day and night.**"**

sure no one was there. I never saw anything. I just dreamed it all, but there was a presence, and it was in that room. It stayed after I turned the light on, and it was up there day and night."

Rachel said she wonders now and then about the yard sale. Who bought the crib. What stories the new owners may have to share.

"I don't know who bought it," she said. "I never felt bad. Who knows if they ever set it up? They may have bought it for a decoration and never put a baby in it.

"But, these things happen to some people and not to others. Who knows why? Maybe part of it is because of how you were raised. They're drawn to you, maybe."

Confusing Cupboard

Joe, a real estate salesman in Raleigh, North Carolina, had gone to the dentist. Over the course of more than seven years, he had become friendly with the dental hygienist and went to her, faithfully, every six months. Her name was Ruth.

Knowing that Joe and his wife were avid antique collectors, Ruth shared a story with him that, he said, contained more than a few unusual occurrences.

"Ruth said she thought I was one of the few people who would believe her and not think that she was completely mad," Joe said. "She also was hoping that I might know of a similar occurrence that I could share with her, and, therefore, make her feel a bit less crazy. Unfortunately for her, I didn't, for I had not run across anything like she experienced."

According to Joe's retelling of her story, Ruth and her husband had bought a quite beautiful antique corner cupboard earlier that year, and they couldn't wait to place it in their dining room.

Ruth spent the first evening that the cupboard was in her house arranging collections of dishes and small figurines on the shelves. She added some heirloom doilies and arranged the entire display in what she considered to be a very artistic arrangement.

Standing back with her arms folded, she admired her work, shut off the dining room light and went upstairs to bed.

The next morning, Ruth hurriedly rushed through the dining room on her way into the kitchen. Casting an admiring glance toward the new cupboard, she stopped suddenly, surprised to see her carefully arranged presentation had been completely changed.

Joe said, "Ruth told me she was surprised because her husband had never before shown the slightest interest in decorating. So she couldn't imagine why he would have rearranged things during the late evening, or early morning, without saying anything to her."

The couple hurried through breakfast and, in the car on the way to work, Ruth asked, "Why in the world did you decide to become a decorator at this late date?" Returning her question with a totally blank stare, the confused husband denied touching anything in the cupboard.

> **❝**He tried to assure her that he was not the phantom decorator in these midnight interior design battles.**❞**

Ruth didn't believe her husband. Sure he was playing a joke, she decided to go along with his scheme and see how long he planned to stretch it out. That night, she rearranged the items in the new cupboard, placing each piece back to where it had been the night before.

The next morning she saw that the items had been moved around again.

Wondering why her husband was playing with her, Ruth rearranged the items again, for a third time.

The next morning, for the third day in succession, the pieces of her collection were rearranged and disturbed.

On the way to work, she told her husband that she was getting tired of his "little game, which wasn't very amusing."

Again, he denied any knowledge of what she was saying and tried to assure her that he was not the "phantom decorator in these midnight interior design battles."

"Ruth admitted," said Joe, "that she sensed her husband was telling the truth. But she was at a loss, since she had no other logical explanation. Nothing else had occurred to her."

After two more days of rearranging and trying to find a reason for the continuing disturbances and mysterious occurrences,

Ruth and her husband had a long talk. He also admitted feeling uneasy, and that convinced her he was telling the truth.

That night, together, Ruth and her husband set up the interior of the cabinet and made a diagram of the way the items were arranged.

The next morning they descended the stairs together, eager to observe the results. As was the case the last few days, the contents of the corner cupboard were changed.

Rather than rearrange the cabinet's contents again, they agreed to leave things alone and, apparently, so did the ghost. Ruth said she decided that the spirit in the cupboard was satisfied with its arrangement of her collection. Also, she admitted that there was no way she could keep moving the articles back into a position that suited her every morning without becoming extremely confused and frustrated.

A few months later, Ruth and her husband attended a party in Durham. Also present was a person who worked in the parapsychology laboratory at Duke University.

After a few drinks, Ruth said she was relaxed enough to share her story. To her relief, the new acquaintance was quite interested and not the least bit surprised or amazed at the story of the mischievous cupboard she had described.

"Ruth said the man told her that what they had encountered was a poltergeist," recalled Joe. "She said he told her it was probably a benign spirit that was more playful than harmful, and that they often were attached to some object to which they had felt a special attachment in life. She said oftentimes that object was a piece of furniture. He also told her that such a playful spirit could be easily subdued."

The man instructed Ruth and her husband to rearrange their cupboard the way they wanted, and then immediately stand directly in front of the piece of furniture and speak to it in a commanding voice, full of authority and control. They were to tell the spirit that they now owned the cupboard and that they were not going to tolerate any more pranks.

"She said the man told her that method was very successful," Joe said. "So they went home and actually put off doing what they had been instructed to do. She said they both felt foolish. But they eventually decided that no one else was around, and no one else would know, so they gave it a try."

Just before going upstairs to bed, Ruth and her husband slowly entered the dining room and approached the cupboard. They quickly rearranged her collections and then firmly and briefly gave the spirit in the cupboard orders not to move any of the articles ever again.

"Ruth said they had a restless and uneasy night, with neither of them getting any solid sleep," Joe said. "In the morning, they raced downstairs together, rushing toward the cupboard. The contents, for the first time since the cupboard had entered their house, were exactly as they had left them the night before. And she said no further unusual events have occurred."

Author's note: When Joe arrived home, he immediately told this story to his wife, Katie. She called her friend, Lindsey, in South Carolina. You can find out the interesting results of that conversation in the next story, the *Sneak in the Piano*.

Sneak in The Piano

Katie admitted that she was enchanted by the story her husband, Joe, had told her about the haunted corner cupboard.

"Everybody loves a good ghost tale," Katie said. "I have a very dear friend, Lindsey, who lives in Spartansburg, South Carolina, and I just couldn't wait to call her and share the story."

Katie and Lindsey had been very close. As next door neighbors for many years, they had shared much of their lives and developed a wonderfully strong friendship. Excitedly, Katie said she called her friend and shared every detail of the ghost tale Joe had brought home from the hygienist.

To her surprise, Lindsey barely responded, did not ask any questions and, actually, ended the long-distance conversation rather abruptly.

Several days after Katie's call to her friend, the telephone rang. Lindsey was on the phone, apologized for her lack of enthusiasm during their last conversation and proceeded to share an unusual tale of her own.

Several years earlier, Lindsey had purchased an upright piano from her next door neighbor.

It had beautiful, ornately carved, light brown wood and fit perfectly in her home. But from the day it entered her house, she was plagued by strange occurrences.

Things would be lost, then reappear. There were unexplained sounds, footsteps.

She would sit in her den, alone, and suddenly feel air stir about her as if someone were walking nearby. Other times, she would smell a particular scent of perfume, but no one else was about.

"One of the first things I noticed about the piano," Lindsey said, "was that sheet music would not stay on the stand. I would always find it on the floor. Every time I walked into the living room, the music was on the floor. And if I would pick it up, put it back on the piano and go into the kitchen, within minutes it would be back on the floor.

"My husband said it was the air currents, or the blower from the air conditioning or heater, but I knew differently. He is a scientist and very practical. Everything has to have a logical explanation. I told him there was something strange going on, but he didn't pay me any mind. He told me never to tell anybody that I thought there was something strange about the piano. In fact, he made me promise never to tell anyone.

"So when Katie called with the story about the cupboard, I wanted to tell her about my piano, but I couldn't. So I listened and got off the phone very quickly," Lindsey said. "It took me several days before I worked up the courage to share these concerns I had about my piano with her. It made me feel better that I could finally talk to someone about it.

"After I opened up to her, I was able to give her updates concerning the little strange events that I noticed. Over the years we'd be in touch. It was just our little secret."

A few years later, near the end of November when Christmas was approaching, Lindsey said she was wrapping a number of presents for her ladies auxiliary group. The dozen items were so small that they could all fit into one large shopping bag.

"Some friends were coming to pick me up for lunch, and I was running late," Lindsey said. "I rushed through the rest of my wrapping, gathered the gifts and materials together and placed them out of the way. Several days later, I just couldn't remember what I had done with the bag of wrapped gifts.

"I was at a loss," Lindsey continued. "All the things I had intended to use as Christmas gifts had just disappeared. I was talking to Katie on the telephone, and she suggested that the piano had taken them. She also said I was going to have to talk to the piano, just like the dental hygienist did to her cupboard, and ask for the presents back."

At first, Lindsey said she thought it was a ridiculous idea, but when the presents didn't turn up after three more days of searching, she agreed to try anything.

She recalled pacing back and forth in front of the piano. "If you don't think I felt like a fool," she said, laughing. "I was nervous. But, I remember how Katie said this approach had solved the problem with the cupboard. So, I finally started talking. I wasn't looking at the piano, but walking back and forth. I said, 'I'm a little bit weary of picking the sheet music up off the floor. . . . And I'd like to have my Christmas gifts back, because it's getting close to the season. I'd also like all this stuff to come to a halt, because my patience is running out.' Then, when I was all finished, I walked out of the room."

"It's difficult telling people that you actually talked to a piano. Some of the looks I get are really incredible—almost as incredible as what actually happened."

Three days later, Lindsey went to the coat closet in the entry hall to get out the vacuum cleaner. She had been in and out of that same closet every day, either to get to the coats or to use the appliance, which was on the floor at the very front of the closet.

"I opened the closet door," Lindsey said, "looked down to get the vacuum cleaner, and I had to move a shopping bag . . . filled with the Christmas presents that I had wrapped weeks before and that had been lost all that time.

"Lo and behold, there they were. But I had been in and out of that closet on a daily basis for weeks. There was no way that bag could have been there, and there was no way I would have not noticed it if it was there.

"I was so surprised. I was just flabbergasted. I raced to the telephone to call Katie and tell her a funny thing happened on the way to the vacuum."

After the presents were returned, Lindsey said there were no further incidents in her home. However, although nearly 10 years have passed since the incidents, she still wonders if her neighbor, from whom she had bought the piano, had any similar experiences.

"I've often wanted to go next door and ask her," Lindsey said, and then added. "If she didn't have any experiences, she would think I was crazy; and if she did know about it being haunted, she would be embarrassed that I knew about it and wondered why she hadn't said something before she sold it to me.

"For a long time I wondered if she looked over at my house and said, 'Aha! I'm glad I got rid of that haunted thing!' "

But then, about three years after the Christmas presents incident, Lindsey's husband came home and announced that he had sold the piano—to the next door neighbor on the other side.

"I was so aggravated with my husband," Lindsey said, "and also amazed that he had sold the piano to our neighbors. I told him 'I wished you hadn't done that,' and he replied, 'There's nothing wrong with that piano. It's just your imagination.' "

As a result of her husband's action, Lindsey was in an interesting and curious position.

In addition to wondering what had occurred to the former owner of her piano, she also was wondering what was going to happen to the new owner of the instrument.

"I was so very interested," she said, "but I never could bring myself to ask the new or the old owners if anything odd resulted from their getting or having had the piano. I've been very curious about that, but I also realize that I'm in the middle, a secret link in the chain of psychic ownership.

"I may never know what incidents happened to the owners of the piano before I got it, or what will happen to those who will care for it after me. But I do know that it hid my Christmas presents and gave them back after I asked for them. It's all been highly unusual, and I don't go out of my way to share all this with others. It's difficult telling people that you actually talked to a piano. Some of the looks I get are really incredible—almost as incredible as what actually happened."

Mysterious Folk Art

Suzanne and James Hofmeister of Buffalo, New York, are serious about antiques. In addition to collecting and dealing, they have been involved in academic research and on-site field studies throughout the country, particularly in the Northeast and American Southwest.

Results of their work have been published in both antique-oriented periodicals and academic journals. Their serious, methodical approach involving the academic aspects of antiques, along with their story and experiences, paint a fascinating and bothersome account of things that go bump in the night.

In the mid-1980s, the Hofmeisters became aware of a certain group of folk art pieces created in the early part of the century by Axel Gustafson, a former carver of pipe organ and piano cases in St. Charles, Illinois.

Gustafson eventually moved to Franklinville, New York, bought a dairy farm and continued his carving, creating a substantial number of life-size lawn sculptures and smaller standing and hanging pieces.

The artworks included numerous life-size animals, such as a free-standing, 6-foot cement giraffe, as well as smaller pieces, including a mounted, 2-foot long and 10-inch high fox. A sculpture of a standing deer was over 6 feet high and nearly as long, while a pair of resting lions each were over 6 feet long and more than 2 feet high.

Many of the larger works were made of wood that had been carved and later coated with a cement overlay. Some of the finished pieces were painted, and a few even featured glass eyes.

The couple had come across several Gustafson pieces here and there, and they were intrigued by the workmanship and the stories associated with the reclusive sculptor.

In a *New York Folklore* article, the Hofmeisters wrote, "According to Illinois relatives and local citizenry, it was a 'sad and lonely' family. They were 'loners,' living apart in their rural setting. Times were hard, and at the beginning of their residency the entire herd of cows contracted tuberculosis and had to be destroyed. All their relatives lent them money to tide them over this crisis, and they struggled for a long time.

"Apparently Axel shunned the heavier work, leaving it for the children to do while he did the lighter work. Carving his animals was his passion, his relaxation year-round. He was described as 'always having a carving knife in his hand.' He evidently carved while doing chores both outside and within the cow barn."

The Hofmeisters eventually tracked the bulk of Gustafson's pieces through records from a country auction in Franklinville in August 1981, held to dispose of the contents of the Gustafson family's modest farmhouse.

Included among the sculptor's works were a standing horse, zebras, a wolf, a bull, eagles, a bear head, moose, oxen and wagon and other assorted standing pieces and wall plaques. Thirty were sold at the auction and 13 more were known to exist elsewhere.

Drawn to the works of the sculptor/farmer who had died in 1945, the Hofmeisters began making trips from their home to the area of New York known as the Southern Tier—around Allegheny and Franklinville—to seek out more pieces, capture them on film, purchase some for themselves and discover the stories behind the works and the artist.

Both Suzanne and James are art teachers and hold master's degrees. Since one of their areas of specialty and interest is folk art, they decided to make the artist and his folk carvings the focus of a study.

The drive from Buffalo to the Southern Tier was about 60 miles, and they made the trip frequently during their quest that consumed an entire summer.

The result was a 15-page article—entitled "Alex Gustafson (1867-1945) Folk Sculptor of Franklinville, New York." Complete with 14 photographs, it appeared in the Vol. XV, Nos. 1-2, 1989 issue of *New York Folklore*, while a shorter version was published in the November 1987 issue of *Maine Antique Digest.*

Suzanne said she and James conducted interviews with people who owned some of the pieces and others who lived in the Franklinville area. There also was some contact with Gustafson's family in Illinois.

"Gustafson's family was very suspicious of us," Suzanne remembered. "They couldn't imagine that these things could have any monetary or cultural value. We eventually were able to talk to them by phone and correspond with them to a degree through the mail.

"But the interesting thing," Suzanne added, pausing as she shared the fact, as if it still puzzled her, "was that we were never able to give them a copy of the finished article. They just moved and disappeared. The phone was disconnected, and there was no forwarding address. It was very unusual."

But, on reflection, the lack of contact seemed to make sense. Especially when one considered the rumors in the Franklinville area about Gustafson, Suzanne said. Comments she heard seemed to indicate that the family was embarrassed because the children were forced to stay on the farm and work to support their father's obsession with carving. Because of their farm chores, they did not receive much formal education. There also were questions about the mysterious death of Gustafson's wife and daughter. It's said they died from drinking poisoned water in the family well.

All of these associated comments and rumors, however, tend to draw one away from the primary focus, Gustafson's creations.

The Hofmeisters own seven of Gustafson's pieces, and they have never experienced anything unusual.

Such is not the case with some other collectors.

Because the farmer who bought the Gustafson property saved all the auction records, it was possible for the Hofmeisters to contact many of the new owners of the sculptures.

The Deer Head, created in the 1915-1920 period, is carved wood that is stained with varnish. The wall hanging is 19 inches high and has real antlers, large eyes and a soft expression.

It was sold to a young couple in Olean, New York. As soon as Suzanne called and talked to the wife it was apparent there was something wrong.

"On the phone," Suzanne recalled, "the wife said to me, 'That piece will never be allowed in my house for as long as I live.'

"They said they brought the piece home and they liked it a lot. At some point, they noticed that the eyes had been painted over by the artist, so they scraped the paint and discovered that they were the type a taxidermist would use.

> **"There seems to be more to the story that is unspoken and hidden behind the doors of the tiny homes and shanties off the backroads and in the hamlets and hollows of the Southern Tier."**

"That's when the couple said, 'We released old Gus' spirit when we scraped off the paint.' "

For no apparent reason, doors began slamming, toilets would flush, lights went on and off and creaking noises were heard throughout the house.

According to Suzanne, the man and wife told her they were very nervous, that they "felt terrified."

Eventually, they discussed calling a priest from nearby St. Bonaventure University, who was an official exorcist, to come to the house. It's not known if the action ever took place. But, the wife said, they moved the Deer Head into the shed, outside of the house.

"The husband," said Suzanne, "intended to take the piece and hang it in their summer cottage. But his wife was adamant that it not be allowed back into the house."

To add more substance to the mysteries that were beginning to surround some of Gustafson's works, that same Saturday James and Suzanne had arranged a meeting 20 miles away to talk to another owner of some pieces sold at the auction.

"We met a dealer who had bought several pieces and who didn't know the other couple we had spoken to that morning," Suzanne said. "And as soon as we mentioned the items, she said, 'I hardly ever want to talk about those ghastly things.'

"From the minute she had brought them into the house, the woman said she and her husband started having nightmares and 'day terrors,' which she described as tremendous anxiety attacks while up and around. She said she couldn't wait to get rid of them."

Within two weeks, the lady had sold all four pieces at a decent profit. But, according to Suzanne, "The woman did not even want to talk about them. She wanted them out of her life and out of her thoughts. She said as soon as they were out of her home things returned to normal. But she maintains today that the pieces were somehow 'evil' and unnatural.

"What really affected me," Suzanne said, "was that here are two different families, 20 miles apart, who had no contact, did not know each other and who had troubling experiences. It was eerie, to put it mildly."

The third and final "unnerving" incident involved Gustafson's 6-foot tall giraffe.

John, a Vietnam veteran, was a well-known "picker" in the Allegheny area. He would travel the backroads, knock on doors and find interesting pieces. Often, he worked with an older friend who also was a picker.

John bought the giraffe and stored it in his friend's barn. Suzanne and James had arranged to meet John and see Gustafson's giraffe sculpture. When they arrived and went with John to his friend's home the giraffe was not there.

The three of them searched two barns and could not discover its whereabouts.

"A few days later," said Suzanne, "John called me and said his friend had hauled the giraffe out into the field and chopped it up and scattered the pieces. John could not determine the reason, or, if he knew, he was unwilling to share it with me.

"John, who had been ill with cancer, passed away later that year. The other man, John's picking friend who had been apparently healthy, died rather unexpectedly of the same type of cancer shortly thereafter. Then, three months after John's death, his house burned to the ground with two Gustafson pieces in it."

The bizarre nature of the series of events is often in Suzanne's and James' thoughts.

"We've talked about it a lot," she said. "It's fascinating and very interesting that these stories came to us from various sources, who had no knowledge of each other. That has validated them as far as we're concerned. I certainly believe what these people have said they've experienced."

Suzanne said she had met another owner of a Gustafson piece who had been afflicted with injuries and illness.

"The Gustafson family was lonely," Suzanne said, "and one gets the impression they were engaged in a struggle for existence. There also may have been some resentment because the children worked and he carved."

In talking to Suzanne, one gets a sense that there's something unsavory about the entire Gustafson story. There seems to be more to the story that is unspoken and hidden behind the doors of the tiny homes and shanties off the backroads and in the hamlets and hollows of the Southern Tier. And although some information about Gustafson's carving and subsequent hauntings has slipped out, much more will never be learned. One can only imagine the secrets buried along with the mysterious, solitary wood carver.

"People really talked when John's house burned to the ground," Suzanne said. "They said it was amazing that the house just couldn't be saved, and there was more talk when the other man died so suddenly. It was like trouble followed trouble all the way down the line."

The Hofmeisters own seven Gustafson works, including the Wolf's Head that the sculptor never took into his house. Apparently, said Suzanne, the sculptor was afraid of wolves and this potent piece was a talisman for him.

"I'm not concerned with the pieces we have," Suzanne said. "Nothing strange has happened to us since we've owned them. But, I must admit, I'm still waiting to run into someone else with another story."

Spats Near the Chair

*A*manda lives outside Chestertown, an historic town in Kent County, Maryland, known for a delightful bookstore across from the town fountain, numerous antique shops and picturesque, tree-lined streets. The area is a mecca for recreational boaters, and a Tea Party reenactment is held each May to commemorate the Colonists' anger against the British in the days leading up to the Revolutionary War.

Now in her 40s, Amanda can recall, as a child, hearing people say that her grandmother had "the second sight."

"My grandmother would tell me that all the time," Amanda said. Now a real estate agent working on the Eastern Shore, she recalls her years spending time with "Grams" with deep affection, listening to her family stories and tales of a different era. The two women from different generations remained very close.

Amanda shared the story of the time that her grandmother was playing alone in the front yard of her home. It was summer, about the time when the sun was going down and darkness was beginning to claim the town.

"She looked up, and she was only about 5 or 6 at the time," Amanda said, "and there was a beautiful woman, with bright gold hair and deep blue eyes, standing at the edge of the wrought-iron fence. Grams said she felt very comfortable with her, and that the lady motioned for Grams to come to her, to follow her outside the fence.

"Grams knew she shouldn't go, but admitted she was tempted. Her father—my great grandfather—had told her not to leave the yard. She said she remembered that the strange woman had on a white blouse and a dark black suit. When she told my great grandfather about the lady and what she was wearing, Grams said he started to cry. It seems that the description was what Grams' mother—who died soon after she was born— looked like and the clothing was what she wore when she was buried."

According to Amanda, her grandmother never saw the woman again, but other things occurred throughout the years.

One incident involved the spats and the chair.

After Amanda's grandfather died, when Grams was older and living alone in Laurel, Maryland, she raced across the living room of a small bungalow to close the windows during a sudden rainstorm.

Near the window stood a platform rocker, made of thick wood, with lion heads carved on the arms. The chair rocks on hidden springs and has heavy upholstery that offers a comfortable back and seat.

"Grams had to step in front of the rocker—and a pair of large legs, with white spats on the feet—to get in front of the window to pull it down. Automatically, she said, 'Excuse me,' to the figure. Then, as she was leaving the room, realized there was a man in the chair!"

When Grams passed on, the chair was sent up to Amanda in Chestertown. She's had it for almost 20 years.

"We used to ask Grams about the story, where the man in the spats came from," Amanda said. "But she had no answers. She wondered herself where those legs came from, and when she would see them again."

> **"**Sometimes, during a thunderstorm, I go in the hall, at the opposite end away from the chair, and just watch and wait.**"**

Today, the 80-year-old platform rocker sits on the second floor of Amanda's 18-room, Victorian home in the center of town. It rests between two large windows, overlooking the front yard and street below.

"It's really a very nice view," she said. "I figure if he's here, he's going to want to see outside. I certainly wouldn't think of putting him up in the attic and out of the way, where he wouldn't have a good view.

"Sometimes, during a thunderstorm, I go in the hall, at the opposite end away from the chair, and just watch and wait. I guess I'd like to see him, sitting there with those spats. It would be some kind of connection with Grams. But, I'm also afraid he'll be there, especially if it starts raining in and I have to go over and close the windows."

Ash Lady

J had met Bill a few years ago, when he told me about a ghostly experience he had witnessed as a child. He also educated me to the wonders and mysteries of healing through "powwowing"—but that's another story for another time.

On this particular afternoon, the "Ash Lady" was the focus of our conversation.

A 75-year-old retiree, Bill sat in his room in Newark, Delaware. A writer himself, his trimmed beard gave Bill an Ernest Hemingway-like appearance. He was articulate and exacting as he eagerly recalled the tale told to him by his mother, which he passed on to me and which I now share with you in his own words.

"My mother was a very religious person," Bill began. "We couldn't have a deck of cards in the house. They were considered implements of the devil. If you knew my mother, she wouldn't tell a lie, ever; and she would not go to her grave having ever let a lie pass her lips.

"My grandmother lived with us, on the East Side of Wilmington—on Spruce or Bennett Street. I was born December 19, 1920. By the time I was about six or seven years old, I had heard the story several times. It happened just before I was born.

"I don't know why, but my mother and grandmother had no fear of ghosts, as most people did then and still do today.

"After World War I, the vets were coming home and a bunch had come off the farms and didn't want to go back. So, during those boom days after World War I, they lingered in the cities and tried to get work. Because there was a shortage of rooms, the local government asked people to take in the vets.

"My mother had a spare room and rented it to two soldiers, Bob and Vincent. In their room there was a used bureau my mother had purchased at Hurlock's Furniture Store. It had a mirror on the top with a number of drawers that pulled out at the bottom.

"Now, this is important. My mother had inadvertently neglected to tell the boarders about the 'Ash Lady.' It was a ghost that my mother and grandmother had seen on numerous occasions. They called her the Ash Lady because she was gray in color, like cool ashes.

"They had seen the ghostly woman because she would come in every night, after you had retired, and rifle through that particular bureau. But, when you looked afterwards, there was nothing disturbed. The ghost wouldn't say anything or look at anyone in the area. Then, she would leave the room and disappear into oblivion. She never came in the daytime, only at night.

"My mother and grandmother were accustomed to the strange visits and appearances. So, they didn't give her a second thought and said nothing to the two strangers, even though the bureau was in their room.

"At breakfast after their first night, one of them asked my mother, 'Excuse me, Mrs., but did you come in our room last night and look in the bureau?'

"My mother said, 'Oh! I forgot to tell you about the Ash Lady.' She apologized, told them the story and offered to put a different bureau in the room so they wouldn't be confronted again.

> **"The ghost wouldn't say anything or look at anyone in the area. She never came in the daytime, only at night."**

"The two men weren't upset. They were more interested in trying to figure out why the Ash Lady was coming into the room and searching the bureau every night.

"One of them suggested the Ash Lady was trying to find something, and he asked if they could inspect the bureau and look for markings or writing or anything that might give a clue.

"My mother and grandmother accompanied them upstairs, and the four of them took the drawers out and turned the bureau upside down. On the bottom of one of the drawers they found a thin sealed envelope. It turned out to be a will—apparently the Ash Lady's will.

"Hurlock's store was only four or five blocks away. So they took the envelope with the will to be returned to the original owners of the bureau.

"It turned out that the furniture people knew the family. They said the owners' mother had died and the family was unable to find the will. They were searching every nook and cranny of her old house. They were notified and came to get the will and were very happy.

"The Ash Lady never returned to our house. Her mission was accomplished. I'm telling you, I believe it to be the truth. And, if you knew my mother, you'd believe it to be the absolute truth."

Danny's Rosary

anny lived the last years of his life in a Wilmington, Delaware, nursing home. A tiny, wiry Irishman, he loved listening to recordings of the Clancy Brothers and other folk singers from the Emerald Isle. Workers and visitors would often hear the spirited and melancholy music as they passed his room on the second floor.

Danny had another interesting trait.

You would never see him without his rosary.

Whether in his room alone or while attending activities in the common areas, you would always see Danny fingering the beads as he silently recited an endless string of Hail Mary's and Our Father's, with a Glory Be thrown in at the end of each decade.

It was a magnificent rosary, given to him by an aunt from the Old Country, he said.

The original black darkness of its rounded wooden beads was worn to a lighter shade from constant use. And the metal crucifix, attached to the small wooden cross, was a fine example of loving craftsmanship, long disappeared from the mass production world of the 20th century.

Diane was the activities director at the nursing home and very close to Danny. The fact that her family was Irish probably accounted for her initial attachment to him.

During the months she worked in the building, their friendship grew. Oftentimes, she would visit with him when she had a few extra minutes. He would give her some of the crafts he made as presents and she would drop off some homemade cookies and small treats in his room from time to time.

It hit her pretty hard when he passed away suddenly. It happened during the evening, when she was off. But in her business, she said, you have to get used to things like that.

"It's part of the job," she said. "The hardest part, at times."

A few months after Danny passed away, a maintenance man was in her friend's old room, cleaning the heater. He had removed the metal screen that covered the unit.

Diane happened to be passing the doorway and walked in.

As she walked toward the opening in the wall, she saw a metal flash on the floor.

"I moved closer, leaned over, and picked it up," Diane said. "I was amazed. It was the crucifix from Danny's rosary. I would have known it anywhere, especially with his initials carved so very carefully on the back."

Smiling, she closed it in the palm of her hand and placed it in her purse.

"I remember thinking how wonderful it was to have this special memento of Danny's to remember him by," Diane explained. "It was almost as if he had left it for me. God knows how the crucifix could have come off the rosary, and how it got back behind the heater. But I didn't care, I was just happy to have it."

> **❝I sort of feel like Danny is with me, and protecting me. It's a comforting feeling. I've thought about the night that it flew off the Bible in my room. ❞**

Apparently, Danny's religious keepsake was a bit more spirited than the average store-bought rosary.

"When I got home that night," Diane said, "I took the crucifix out of my purse and placed it on my night stand. Later, before I went to bed, I picked it up, held it a moment, said a prayer for Danny and then set it down on the top of my Bible, that I have near my bed.

"I jumped up immediately, for the crucifix flew—I mean flew, not slid, literally flew—off the Bible and landed on the floor. At first I thought I was crazy, so I picked it up and placed it in the same spot again, and it did the same thing. Flew off into the air and landed on the floor."

After standing speechless for about a minute, Diane said she picked the object up, held it in her hand and yelled at her unseen visitor.

"I knew it was Danny," she said, "so I told him that if he wanted to stay he was welcome, but he'd have to behave."

Nothing more has happened since then.

Diane pulled the crucifix from her purse and gently placed it on an end table.

"I keep it with me all the time," she said. "I sort of feel like Danny is with me, and protecting me. It's a comforting feeling. I've thought about the night that it flew off the Bible in my room. I've decided that it was his way of letting me know he was around, and that he's glad I found it and that I have it. And I'm glad, too."

Hexed Ring

Karen of Micanopy, Florida, admitted that she has no special interest in antiques. It's her sister, Sharon, who is the real collector of the clan, dabbling in antiques, family history and family memorabilia. Sharon lives in Grove City, Pennsylvania, in the western end out near Pittsburgh.

That's where the ring is.

Safely out of touch, resting in a box in the bottom of a dresser drawer.

It's yellow gold. Very old.

Karen said the stone is a red garnet, and smooth on top. A little gold flower is embedded in the flat surface of the red stone. The ring is small, only about the size of a girl's high school class ring.

The ring was in the family for years and belonged to Aunt Hattie, Karen and Sharon's great aunt.

After Aunt Hattie passed away, the two sisters joined their mother at her home to help sort through Aunt Hattie's belongings.

Karen recalled the events that occurred more than 25 years ago.

It was a bright afternoon in the western part of the Keystone State.

"I remember Sharon opening up the jewelry box," said Karen, "and she saw the ring and said, 'That's pretty. Can I have it?' Mother gave it to her and Sharon wore it almost every single day. As I recall, she wore both Aunt Hattie's garnet ring and another one that belonged to our grandmother."

In 1990, a group of women from Sharon's work gathered at a friend's house where a psychic named Brenda was scheduled to give readings. All of the participants had been instructed to bring a special personal object along that they could give the psychic to hold.

Sharon took Aunt Hattie's ring.

When she gave the ring to Brenda, the psychic said the wearer was a member of the Order of the Eastern Star.

The psychic's statement was true. Aunt Hattie had indeed been an active member of that organization.

According to Karen, "The psychic then told Sharon that, 'There were the souls of dozens of children, both born and those who had lived short lives, inside that ring.' She also said the original wearer of the ring had been very sad because she had no children or because of the death of her children."

After checking family history, Karen discovered that Aunt Hattie had had several pregnancies. Three were full-term pregnancies that resulted in two stillbirths and the live birth of a set of twins. But, one of the twins died a few weeks after birth; the other child died at the age of two.

"That evening at the session," Karen said, "the psychic told my sister that 'Whoever wore that ring would never have children unless it was ritually cleansed.' "

"Who can say who or what came first . . . the death of the children or the souls in the ring?"

Proper cleansing would involve a blessing by a priest, who should leave the ring in a container of Holy Water overnight. The second suggested method was to put the ring in a bowl filled with water and let it stay out overnight under a full moon.

According to Karen, her sister did neither. She just put Aunt Hattie's ring in a box in her drawer, and that's where it remains.

"For about two years prior to the psychic session," Karen said, "my sister had been trying to become pregnant, even going to a fertility clinic weekly for treatments. It was at a university that was about a two-hour drive away. And up to that time she had no luck at all getting pregnant.

"But after talking to Brenda, Sharon put the ring away, never wore it again, and she became pregnant soon afterwards. She now has two children."

According to Karen, no one in the family knows where the ring came from. It is believed to have been an anniversary gift from Uncle Clarence to Aunt Hattie. All anyone can remember, she added, is that he got it somewhere in Pennsylvania.

"I come from a family of pack rats," Karen said. "My grandmother said if grandpa died first, she was going to light a match to the house and barn and let it all burn down and leave. Unfortunately, she died first and all the stuff that had been collected was left behind.

"No one is left who remembers anything or can give us any information that would help solve the mystery of the ring," said Karen. "No one knows if Aunt Hattie was the first wearer or not. And who can say who or what came first, the death of the children or the souls in the ring?

"I do know that my sister still has it, and that it hasn't been cleansed. But I tell you this, I would hope she would get it cleansed before she passes it along to her daughter."

What's In a Picture?

*E*lisabeth is a housewife and floral designer in St. Leonard, Maryland, a small town located on the Western Shore not far from the Chesapeake Bay. In her mid 30s, she is a collector of Civil War ambrotypes and daguerreotypes. She explained that a daguerreotype is a picture printed on metal through a technique that was popular in the early to mid 1800s. Ambrotypes were made by a different process, resulting in a glass negative backed by a dark surface so the image would appear as a whitish positive. Often, the fragile images are found in small, book-like folders made of leather and padded for safekeeping.

For decades, these objects were stored in attics, cellars and sheds. Eventually, they started to appear at flea markets, rummage sales and second hand shops.

Recently, however, with increased interest in the pieces themselves—and any items related to the Civil War—both ambrotypes and daguerreotypes have become harder to find— and they have become much more expensive.

"I started collecting them about seven years ago," Elisabeth said. "I have about 100 that I display and keep in a great big Civil War album. I'm fascinated with the Civil War, and I have both Union and Confederate soldiers. When I started out, you could get an ambrotype for about $5 to $10. Now, you can't find them for under $50, anywhere; and it's not unusual to pay $125 for only one.

"The people who posed for an ambrotype used to have to sit for about a half hour. They couldn't smile or make the slightest move. No one could hold a smile that long, plus it was uncomfortable. That's why they're not smiling."

Elisabeth explained that it's always been hard to find Confederate soldiers. More of them were killed and they had less money than their Union counterparts to spend on such a frivolity as having one's picture taken.

While visiting her parents on Tilghman Island, on the Eastern Shore, Elisabeth was browsing in an antique shop and noticed an ambrotype. It was not a soldier, so she didn't buy it. But, something kept telling her to go back and get it.

"For some reason, the man in the ambrotype I didn't buy kept creeping in my thoughts, and that night I even dreamed about it. So the next day, I went back and I had to buy it.

"It's a man, sitting there," she said. "He is dressed in the style of the 1850s, when men wore heavy overcoats and formal clothing. I took it out of the case to clean it. But, when I removed the back, there was a tintype of a Civil War soldier, a Confederate, about the same size as the image I had bought.

"I thought, 'Oh, my God! I hit the jackpot!' Especially, finding a Confederate soldier. I only spent $10 and, considering it was a tintype of a Confederate, it was worth at least $100. I was in total shock. I told some of my friends and they couldn't believe my luck."

Elisabeth purchased a sturdy, sculptured glass frame for the soldier. She explained that when tintypes are exposed to the air the gold begins to turn green.

"They can't be exposed to the sun, bright lights or air, or the image will fade," she said.

An antique secretary in Elisabeth's living room is one of the places she displays her finds. She decided to keep the newfound ambrotype and daguerreotype on the same shelf—the man was on the left and the soldier was about a foot away, to the right.

"Soon after I set them up," she said, "no matter what I did, the ambrotype sat there, but the Civil War soldier would turn to face the man—the older man in the ambrotype that I found the Confederate image behind.

"I had them on the same level, facing out so I could see them easily as I passed by. But each time I looked the soldier was turned, like he was looking to the side at the man in the ambrotype.

"At first, I thought one of the kids got in there, or it just hadn't happened—that it was my imagination. But, I know how I set

40

them up, and I had to fix it a couple times a week. And it still happens. I've been collecting these things for six years and nothing like this ever happened before. I told my mother about it, but she wasn't surprised."

Elisabeth took the images with her to Baltimore, where she visited a female psychic. After holding them, the clairvoyant said that the father's name was John, and he had been a dentist. The boy was his son, and his name was Alan. The psychic believed that Alan was killed in the Civil War and the man had also lost his wife from a disease during the war.

The psychic said she believes that the man was very depressed and he lost everything he had during the Civil War. He originally placed the son's picture behind his, "so they could always be together."

The psychic also mentioned that the father eventually committed suicide, perhaps to be reunited with his family.

"I wasn't really surprised," Elisabeth said. "That kind of stuff happens. I just figure the father, he wants his son back behind him. But I want him in a frame, so he doesn't get messed up. The psychic told me to put the son back behind his father. When she said that, I got chills so bad!"

> **66** I had them on the same level, facing out so I could see them easily as I passed by. But each time I looked the soldier was turned, like he was looking to the side at the man in the ambrotype. **99**

Elisabeth said she wonders often about the lives and deaths of the people in her collection of 19th-century images. What are their names? Did the soldiers die in the Civil War? Which ones returned home and had children and grandchildren? Did any of then live near her present home? Had she encountered any of their descendants?

41

She also knows that the majority of her questions will never be answered.

"But the father and son, they're my two special ones," she admitted, "just because of what the psychic told me. It's so sad and so strange."

One wonders when the last time the restless spirit of the young man in the gray uniform moved his image, to get a better view of his father.

"Just the other day," she said. "Just the other day."

Talking Candlestick

Sydney is a witch. A follower of Wicca would be a more precise way to describe her. But she quickly pointed out that she is not one to cast spells and she doesn't belong to an organized group, or coven as they are called.

Instead, she considers herself one with nature, follows the passing of the four seasons and communicates with other independent Wicca followers through traditional letters and electronic mail.

The events surrounding her candlestick started at the end of 1993 and lasted into the spring. That's when a New York City penpal, whom Sydney had never met, sent a Yule season gift to her townhouse located near Whitemarsh, east of Baltimore.

Sydney doesn't recall what gift she sent her friend in return, but she does remember receiving the black, ceramic candlestick.

She described the object as a modern, ceramic piece that someone had recently made, probably from a standard greenware mold that could be purchased in any ceramic shop.

The candle holder sat on a saucer-type base, with a small loop that was useful when it was carried.

The candlestick was black, with tiny blue flecks scattered all over the surface, sides and base.

Sydney, who is 35 and makes her living as a writer, said she placed the candlestick on her bedroom dresser, the same piece of furniture she sometimes uses as an altar.

"My son was the first one who noticed the noise," Sydney said. "It was unusual, a soft clicking or popping. At first, I thought it was a coincidence. I'd never had an object do anything like that before. I told my husband about it and he didn't believe me."

As weeks passed, the frequency of the clicking increased.

"It sounded like someone tapping a fingernail against it, but from the inside," Sydney said. "I tried to duplicate the sound from the outside in a lot of different ways, but nothing I did worked. I couldn't make that exact same sound.

"Sometimes, it seemed like the clicking was coming from inside a box. It was a very unusual sound."

Eventually, Sydney's husband admitted he heard the clicking. When it occurred in the middle of the night, he would wake her in bed.

"He'd say, 'It's clicking again. Go and see what it wants,' " Sydney recalled. "I'd walk over to it and say, 'Hello,' and then try to carry on a conversation. I never asked it anything of importance. I didn't know how to get information from it, or ask it a question that it could answer."

Over a period of four months, in early 1994, the black candlestick would constantly try to attract someone's attention, frequently in the evening. Even as persons passed through the bedroom, or simply walked down the hallway, they could hear the distinctive clicking sound.

"I'd pause and say, 'Hello!' " Sydney said. "I always tried to acknowledge it."

She also asked the force within the candlestick if it wanted to be seen and how it was feeling, general type questions that might stimulate a conversation.

> **❝ We don't know if it was because of the rituals or from things we acquire here. But none of it bothered me. ❞**

"I'd ask: 'Do you like us?' and 'Are you having fun?' Other times I'd say, 'I hear you,' and 'What's going on?' I inquired if it was a boy or a girl, or even a fairy, but I got no understandable response, just a clicking in reply."

Sydney paused, smiled, then admitted. "And then, some-times, I'd ask myself, 'Am I losing my mind sitting here talking to a candlestick, or is there really something here?' Besides, with no frame of reference or system of communication, there was no way of even knowing if it was saying a simple yes or no."

Apparently, the tapping candlestick was not the only thing odd in the family's Whitemarsh home.

Sydney said there were other things that happened there, including strange footsteps, lights going on and off unexpectedly and the fact that no one could stay inside the house for even a short amount of time without becoming uneasy.

"We felt comfortable there," she said, "but no one else did. We were open to the release and presence of spirits that needed somewhere to go, and I guess the spirits could sense that, too. That's why they came there.

"Our cat was running around chasing tiny floating points of light. We had several people notice images against glass and pic-tures. We don't know if it was because of the rituals or from things we acquire here. But none of it bothered me.

"None of the small rituals we had in the house were of a sensational nature. They were very calm and benign. I always felt there is a fine line between us and the spirit world, and that we walk in it constantly. I don't think it's out of the ordinary to experience what some people consider to be unusual occur-rences anywhere you go."

Sydney believed the lady who sent her the candlestick may have picked it up in a shop that specialized in selling items asso-ciated with Wicca.

"Whether she did something to it, or whether the candlestick picked up some unusual force by being in the shop for a period of time, I'll never know.

"But the strange thing is, after I wrote her about the noise, I never heard from her again. That was my last contact. I tried to contact her time and time again, but I got no response. I some-times wonder if she knew about the clicking and wanted to get rid of it, so she sent it to me."

Did Sydney believe that the candlestick is haunted?

"There definitely was something attached to it," she said. Then, thoughtfully, she added, "I don't like to use the word 'haunted.' I have friends who have contact with spirits, and they have mentioned to me that neither they or the spirits they communicate with approve of that particular word. It has misleading and negative connotations. I'd rather just say there is much more to it than meets the eye, or the ear, in this case."

Sydney's family moved to her current home in a small suburban development, just outside Washington, D.C., in April of 1994. Nothing has happened since then, and the candlestick has stopped sending signals.

Before the end of the interview, Sydney added one additional tidbit of information.

The candlestick was placed on her dresser, which she used for her rituals. While candles play a major role in many Wicca ceremonies, Sydney had never placed a candle in the haunted holder, and she never used the gift in a Wicca-related activity.

Was it possible the candlestick was signaling that it wanted to have a more active and meaningful role in Sydney's life?

"I never thought of that," she said, "I never used a candle in it, even when I was conducting a number of rituals. That's an interesting point. I might just give it a try."

Who Do Dat VooDoo?

His name was Sailor—that's all, nothing more. He said he didn't want me using his full name, because, as he explained, "I don't want a bunch of nuts like you comin' around, askin' me about ghosts and all that other crap."

We met at the back table of a nameless bar in South Philly. It was a neighborhood place, cozy with small tables and a juke box. The long, thin shuffleboard stood against the wall on the opposite side of the room. From the filled ashtrays and a gathering of empty longneck soldiers standing on the edge of the hardwood, it seemed that the table had not seen any sporting action for the last few days.

Several back issues of the *National Enquirer* and the daily paper were tossed across a few chairs in the corner, for the regulars' use, no doubt. There was old-fashioned tile on the floor—black and white boxes heading off in diagonal streaks that disappeared under dark, knotty-pine paneled walls.

We sat at Sailor's table. Apparently, he lived in the gin mill watching daylight turn into darkness six days a week. He just went back to an empty house to feed his parrots, check the mail and sleep, then returned to the bar every morning no later than 9:30.

He conducted all his business from his small, single-tabled office. Booked a few numbers, sorted out his lottery tickets, watched the news on the tube and conversed with the other regulars. Oh, and, of course, downed quite a few brews and consumed those high calorie, floating-in-fat meals that were absolutely delicious.

Sailor was about 6 feet tall and his skin was dark tan.

Somebody said he used to pilot boats in the Delaware Bay. Another story said he did some charter fishing work and treasure hunting in the Outer Banks and off the coasts of South America and Africa. Nobody knew for sure. Nobody really cared.

Others said they heard he once had a crew searching around the Jersey marshes, looking for Blackbeard's lost treasure. But, anybody with an ounce of brains wouldn't ask Sailor about it, not if they wanted to keep their bones all in one piece.

In his late 50s, he had a grizzled look that was accented by his gray beard. He wore his thinning hair slicked back, obviously using a liberal amount of Wildroot, or its 1990s equivalent. A heavy man, in his hand was an ever-present glass of ice, drowning in cheap—but tasty—bar whiskey. An opened 12-ounce, dark brown beer bottle sat nearby, within easy reach of his right paw in case he needed a quick chaser.

"Let's get somethin' straight," Sailor snapped. "I'm only talkin' to ya because you're a friend of Nick's. If he didn't tell me you were okay, I wouldn't look at you if you were dyin' in front of me on the street."

I nodded and thanked Sailor for his kindness.

"Now, let me tell you something else. I ain't superstitious. I don't believe in that crap, never did, never will. But," he added, with a smile that showed off two faded gold teeth, "I know a hellava lot about that crap."

He went on to explain that the story was mainly about his buddy, Rags, who years earlier had come into contact with a voodoo doll. And that old doll that Sailor eventually bought was the same one he had in his possession at that very minute— inside a paper bag, sitting underneath our table.

"You wanna drink?" Sailor asked.

"No thanks," I said, explaining I was there to work, and, besides, I had to drive.

"Fine," he snapped, adding, "you drive and I'll drink." Smiling, he waved the bartender over to fill up his glass with more dark brown liquid.

After declining several more free drinks, I started to take notes as Sailor related the tale.

Rags owned a small family restaurant south of Chester and he was very superstitious.

How superstitious was he?

"Damn serious superstitious," snapped Sailor, "but then he

was a gambler, and they're all mixed up in that stuff. Hell! Rags wouldn't walk under a ladder, he got scared if you walked in his place with an umbrella that was closed up. Didn't have to even open it. I saw him shoot a whole family of black cats that had taken up residence in a old trashcan behind his place. I tell ya, that man is serious superstitious.

"He used to have his own voodoo doll. Kept it in the kitchen of his place and would stick pins or nails in the damn thing's head for good luck. I swear, I seen him do it."

One day, Rags was talking to a customer at the register in his store, saying he was having a run of bad luck. Rags said the only thing that seemed to help was when he shoved a pin in the head of the homemade voodoo doll that he kept out back. But that was before somebody stole his little creature. He didn't know what happened to it. But since it disappeared, things were really bad lately.

A few minutes later, a young black woman, who had been having lunch at a nearby booth, went up to Rags. She said she had overheard what he said about his voodoo doll. Then she told him that she had one, too, hanging in her bedroom.

The woman asked Rags if he wanted to see it.

"Getting real nervous," said Sailor, "Rags tells her no, that he doesn't want no curse on him. But he has a friend—me—who knows how to handle that stuff and that I'd take a look at it.

"Rags told me he was just agreeing with her, thinking she was crazy," Sailor continued, "but two days later she brings it in, inside a brown paper bag. Now Rags is scared to death, and he won't even look in the bag, let alone touch the damn thing. So he calls me on the phone and says, 'I got this voodoo doll in here! Come on down!'

"Well, I go in his place, he takes me in the back and then points to the bag. He won't even look in at it. I tell ya, he wouldn't touch that doll for a hundred bucks—no—not for all the tea in Commie China. So I pick up the bag and toss it to him, but he runs away. It was a riot. Then, I open up the top and peek inside. There it is, way down in the bottom, a tiny, 6-inch little doll. I thought it was a little kid's hand puppet. But the shape is made out of old fashioned material, and it's got about 60 pins shoved in it.

"I ask what the woman wants for it, a bottle of wine,

money? Rags, he says he don't know. So I give him 20 bucks to give to the woman, and I take my new treasure home with me."

Sailor took a sip from his drink, leaned forward, and said, "You think I'm making this up, don't ya?"

I smiled and said I believed him. He gave me a glare, took a few moments to think about where to lead next with his story. I could tell he was playing with me, dragging the yarn out and not offering to open the bag and show me the doll. I was a captive audience, and a new one that hadn't heard his tales. I knew this would be a long interview, so I waited for him to continue.

"When I picked up the doll with my own hands, after I got home," Sailor said, "the hair on my arms stood straight up. It happened.

"It was flat, like that," he said, pushing his hair down, close against his forearm. Then, he pulled the dark hair, to make it stand up. "I didn't imagine it. It happened, looked just like that. That thing was full of energy, and I saw it."

Sailor ordered another round for himself, then sipped on his drink and started to explain the background of the doll, how it was made, what steps went into its creation.

> **❝**I'd have my own little monster of you, hanging in my cellar. Stick pins in it whenever I was in the mood and watch you jump. What do you think of that? **❞**

"I wasn't there," he said. "So I can just imagine. But, whoever made it, let's just say it was a woman. I'd say she took his picture and set it there, in front of her, as she cut up the clothing. Whether it was his underwear or T-shirt or First Communion suit, it don't really matter. But it had to be something that touched the skin of his body and was truly his very own.

"Then, she cut it out, to form a little person, made the feet, arms and the little head. She took his shoestring, tied a knot to make a noose and tightened it around his neck, like she was strangling him.

"That's important, the symbolic hanging of the person that you hate so much. Then she cut out his head from the picture, a black and white photograph, and glued or pinned it to the face of the doll.

"Finally, the best part, the part where she focused all her thoughts and anger and hatred and stuck the figure with pins. Many, many pins. Through the body, the head, the arm, the legs, the crotch . . . and even the eyes of his photograph.

"She must have had a deep hate for this gentleman, whose picture we will see here today, in this bag. Who knows how long ago the doll was made, and for how long she kept him in the cellar sticking pins into him. Did she do it each night? Only when he made her mad? Was he a boss, neighbor, relative? Who the hell knows? Who the hell really cares? But the fact is, we got him now."

Sailor paused again, getting a refill on his liquid refreshment and obviously satisfied with his last speech.

I asked him why he took the doll. He could have just looked at it and walked away. What was his interest?

"That's a very good question. I take unique things. I like things that are different. I have my own museum, in the cellar of my home. I like mummies and skeletons. But I'm not a man that's superstitious, just curious."

Smiling, Sailor reached into his pocket and pulled out two metal pieces and tossed them onto the table. They clanged as they hit the surface and slid toward me. I saw they were silver colored, old and very stained and rusted. Each piece had a flat, oval-shaped body with two rectangular square pegs protruding upward.

"Know what they are?" he asked. His voice a challenge. His face set in a smile of delight.

I picked one up. It was heavy. Its edges were ragged, uneven. Obviously it was quite old and was worn down by the elements.

"I don't know, some kind of drawer or furniture handles," I guessed.

Lighting up a cigar, he took a puff and smiled. "Not bad. In a sense, you might consider them furniture handles. Well, you were close, real close, but no cigar," he said, laughing, waving his stogie at me.

"Coffin handles! Straight outta an old grave over on Tangier Island. My buddy is a grave digger and he got them off a 1700s coffin. There's a real live ghost story for you. What do you think about that?"

"Well, to tell you the truth, Sailor, they're the only genuine 1700s coffin handles I've come across this week," I said.

My host laughed, then immediately got quiet and thoughtful again.

"You got a sense of humor. I like that," he said, pointing at me with his cigar. "I should take you down into my museum. We could spend hours, no days, down there." He lowered his voice. "I've got stuff you wouldn't believe, and probably some stuff you wouldn't recognize. A few gargoyles, old coins, animal pelts. Even got a real graveyard tombstone."

"Maybe some other time," I said. "Now, when do I get to see the doll?"

"In a few minutes. We're waiting for somebody."

"Who?" I asked.

"A friend. He'll be here soon."

"Does he know about the doll?"

"Hell, yes, he knows. He's the one who I got it from!"

Within a few minutes, Rags entered the front door of the saloon. He walked directly to our table that served as Sailor's daytime office. We exchanged introductions and he pulled over a chair, waiting for Sailor's instructions.

"Tell him the story, Rags," said Sailor, obviously wanting to make sure that I believed what he had told me earlier.

Rags' version matched what I'd been told, but his information on his own doll was particularly interesting.

"Now this was about 20 years ago, so I might be a bit hazy on all the details," Rags said. "But you'll get the idea. Anyway, who's gonna argue with me? Ya know what I mean?"

I nodded and Rags continued. "I had been having a runna bad luck. Didn't hit no numbers. None of my horses are comin' in. I even got sick a lot, more than was usual. So I went out and got this store bought doll. Looked like a cheap kewpie doll, kind you'd win at the carnival for throwin' bottles—nothin' special.

"I had it in the kitchen, and put a nail through it, right through its head. And when I did that, I said, out loud, 'Here's for the no good so and so who's trying to put a hex on me. May it go back on him, and I wish it to be bad luck on him, 10 times over what I got.' "

Rags, paused, took a sip from his beer and looked straight across the table at me. "After I did that, I hit the number the very next day. Next, I picked the horses at the track--three winners in a row. Then, I hit on the number again. Everything I did was up. I had good luck everywhere I turned. It stayed that way for a couple of years. Then, somebody stole my damn doll, and my luck changed bad and the hex started getting bad all over again. That doll," Rags smiled and shook his head, "that little lady, she was my good luck charm. Every time I had a bad day, I'd just put another pin or nail in her head and things would get better."

Rags finished his beer. He and Sailor talked about a few issues of personal importance and he excused himself, probably not wanting to be around when Sailor opened up the bag.

"See that," Sailor said, proudly. "Just like I told you, right?"

I agreed with a nod and weak smile.

Certainly satisfied that Rags had backed up his story, I could see Sailor starting to bend over, reaching toward the floor. The paper rustled as the top of the brown bag was opened.

"So, now it's time to see the monster," he said, offering an evil laugh that sounded like it began somewhere far below his belt.

Slowly, he brought the small, gray, folded papers up and placed them on the center of the table. Carefully, he moved his half-filled drink glass and empty beer bottle aside.

Sailor smiled like a proud father as he unfolded the faded tissue paper that protected his creature's delicate frame.

I looked.

It was tiny. No more than 5 inches high, less than 3 inches wide. A dark shoestring served as a noose-like hanging string. The monster's body was made of cloth, heavy material like old-fashioned underwear that had been cut into the shape of a little person. A faded white Gumby made of cloth looked up at us with no eyes, finger or toes.

But there were legs and arms and a head. The neck was outlined by the tight knot of the dark shoestring. A carefully cut-out face—once part of a faded, black-and-white photograph—was attached to the voodoo doll's head. The photo was connected by several pins that pierced directly through the image's eyes.

There had to be at least 40 more pins stuck into the body. Through the head, arms, legs, crotch, face. Everywhere.

The sharp objects had been shoved in their places so long ago that they were rusted. You could see shiny metal only where the pins had been inside the cloth and had not been exposed to the air.

Sailor seemed proud of his treasure, smiling at me as I slowly examined it from every angle. He handed me a magnifying glass, so I could see more detail.

"It's amazing," I said.

He nodded, pride was obvious on his face.

"You can make one," he said.

"What?" I asked.

"You. . . . You can have one. A beast, a fiend, a *monster*," he smiled after uttering the word, then added, "of your very own."

I looked at him, not knowing what to say.

"Do you hate anyone?"

"Sure, everyone does," I said.

"Then we can make one for you."

I remained silent as he continued talking, explaining how you needed to get some clothing from your enemy. Take it and cut the cloth into the shape of a doll, no more than 14 inches tall, preferably 6 to 10 inches high.

Sailor spoke of the inner physical feelings associated with true hatred, about how to focus one's anger on the image of an enemy.

"Each time you concentrate on that person with loathing," he said, "you stick the doll and the pain is transferred. The shoestring symbolizes being hung, and the picture allows you to see your enemy and concentrate on him."

Closing his eyes, his voice became eerie, as if Sailor was generating the image of a special enemy of his own. His hands faced up, like a pair of hungry claws.

I listened and watched it all, as he continued.

"You have to take all of the hate in your body and throw it at the image of your enemy," he said. "Voodoo is like a religion. It is serious. It is taught from the beginning, when you are born. It only works if you believe in it and respect its strange power. It is not designed to kill quickly, but is made to curse, to hurt over a long period of time. It can give a person an incurable disease, cause him to have an accident, have bad luck fall upon him like rain. All cultures have their own curses. Voodoo, with its dolls, is only one of many ways to summon the spirits to do your evil will."

It was getting close to the time that I should leave. I asked Sailor if he'd ever had any bad luck after owning the doll.

"No! Not one bad time at all," he said. "Probably because I don't believe. But, as I told you, I've studied the black arts and I've witnessed its power."

I started to get up and thanked Sailor for his help, mentioning how much I had learned.

We shook hands. Then, before I made my getaway, he stared straight at me and said, "I could make a voodoo doll of you."

I wasn't prepared for this farewell, so I kept quiet and waited to find out if there was more.

"I could take your shoelaces," he said, pointing at my feet. His voice was harder, evil, more serious than it had been all afternoon. His words were filled with malice. "Then I'd find out where you live and go through your trash and get a piece of your clothes. I'd get your picture, somehow. It's not hard. Use a telephoto camera. No problem.

"But, if I really wanted to get your basic, true energy, the real essence of your spirit, I'd go to your barbershop and steal your hair off the floor. Then, I'd put all the parts together and have my own little monster of you, hanging in my cellar. Stick pins in it whenever I was in the mood and watch you jump. What do you think of that?"

I didn't have an answer. What does one say when he's being told that he's about to be the object of a curse?

Sailor's bold laughter broke the uneasy silence. "Lucky for you I'm not serious, though," he said. "I'm just an old drunk, a pirate talking through his booze. But, hey," he said, patting me on the shoulder, "don't forget to send me a copy of the book that has my story."

I smiled. "Sure. No problem."

Then, as I walked toward the door, I turned, waved and left the bar, thinking, *"I sure hope Sailor likes the way his story turns out."*

SUITS WITH SPIRIT

"**I** don't feel comfortable in modern day clothing. I think it's hideous and doesn't have any character. I'm very theatrical. I like to wear period clothing, hats with feathers and dark lipstick. When I walk into a place, I want people to think I'm from another era."

These are some of the reasons Sandrea, a resident of Annapolis, Maryland, is attracted and attached to period, vintage clothing.

For the past 25 years, since she was 15, she has been collecting pieces that have become part of her extensive, specialized wardrobe, consisting primarily of items from the early 20th century and the 1940s.

During her weekend travels, Sandrea stops in at resale, specialty and consignment shops, antique outlets and Goodwill and Salvation Army stores seeking additions to her wardrobe.

"Prices have risen dramatically in the last few years," Sandrea said, "but sometimes I can get a nice piece cheaply if it needs some minor repair. I bought a 1940s beaded dress recently and it turned out wonderfully."

Selecting a piece of clothing seems to have as much to do with the article as it does with Sandrea's preference.

"Sometimes I think the clothes have spirits attached to them," she said. "I think the persons who had the coat or dress wanted me to have it because they know I will take care of it."

Her current collection includes about 200 articles she wears in public. Only a few are what she would consider collector pieces.

"Among my favorites is a Victorian coat made in 1915. I wear it with gloves and set my hair up so it's appropriate for the manner of that period. I also have a 1940s Tyrolean-type jacket, from Vienna. It has an ornate exterior. It belonged to my mother and I think that's one of the reasons that it's so special.

"But it's so hard to select some over others. Each piece has its own character, and when I wear it I love it."

> **"Sometimes I think the clothes have spirits attached to them. I think the persons who had the coat or dress wanted me to have it because they know I will take care of it."**

There have been a few unusual experiences that Sandrea attributes to articles of clothing.

A red, 1940s dress had the annoying habit of riding up her legs while she was attending a family Thanksgiving dinner. The material seemed to be clinging to her body and, despite her efforts to hold it down, continued to move up above her knees—apparently on its own.

"I was sort of amused," Sandrea said. "I had the feeling that the person who owned it before was a playful type of person.

"When I got home," she added, "I hung it up on the closet door. I do that because I enjoy looking at my clothing. The dress was near a tall floor lamp, and I heard a sound and the dress was brushing against the shade of the lamp.

"When I kept hearing the noise and seeing it move, I called my sister into the room. She saw what was happening and shouted, 'That dress is haunted!' She ran over, smacked the dress with a pillow and said, 'Listen here, ghost. You leave my sister alone!' And it stopped and nothing has happened with that dress since then."

While visiting New Hope, Pennsylvania, Sandrea discovered a wedding dress, made around the turn of the century.

It was embedded with lace roses and very delicate. Because it was dirty and needed some work, the price was only $40.

"I took it home and worked on it," she said. "While I was washing and drying it, I kept getting a creepy feeling, like the former owner was agitated.

"I kept it on the dining room chair overnight, to dry out. That night, I awoke about 2 in the morning. I heard noises, like someone was walking around the house making snoring sounds or snorting like a pig.

"I went back to sleep and was awakened again. This time there was a rustling sound and the snorting again. I knew it wasn't my imagination."

The next night, with the dress still resting in the dining room, the sounds continued. Sandrea folded her find and placed it in a box in the bedroom closet. That night, she and her boyfriend experienced the beginning of two straight weeks of horrifying nightmares.

"He had never had nightmares before," Sandrea said, "and neither had I. I decided it might be from the energy in the dress. For some reason, I shut the closet doors and the nightmares stopped. But, to this day, if I accidentally leave the closet doors open, we have terrible nightmares again. So we check to make sure the doors are shut."

Sandrea said she's very sensitive to psychic sensations. When she's in a shop and gets a negative feeling she won't buy a piece.

A 1930s black velvet dress with sequins and beads proved the exception to Sandrea's rule.

"I found it bundled up in a creepy garage in New England," she said. "The bad vibes just jumped right out at me, but because it was so beautiful I bought it. I had bad headaches all the way home from the trip, but at first I didn't associate them with the dress.

"When I got home, I aired it out. I got the feeling that it didn't like being touched or bothered with. Like when you enter into a room and you notice someone with animosity toward you. I said some prayers and tried to get rid of the anger by airing it out."

As with the white wedding dress, Sandrea said she began experiencing nightmares and also headaches. She was tempted to put the dress in a bag and give it to Goodwill, but she just couldn't let it go.

"I ended up talking to it. I said, 'Listen, dress. I like that black dress and I'm going to hang it up in the closet and keep her.'

"I put it in the closet with the other clothes, and I think they've absorbed some of its power. Its strength has dissipated quite a bit. But, I must admit, I haven't worn it yet."

It's Sandrea's opinion that much of her clothing has energy that has been transferred from the original wearer.

"I think that clothes retain some of the characteristics, or energy—whether it be good, happy, evil, patient—of the wearer. No matter how old it is, the garment always retains a part of that primary energy, and that's what makes old clothes so fascinating."

Sandrea said she does notice interesting reactions when people learn of her attitudes toward her clothing collection.

"Most people find my ideas amusing," she said. "They don't take them very seriously because a lot of them haven't had anything like this happen to them. It's hard for them to understand or relate to. But, if you've had an unusual experience yourself, what I describe is so much more meaningful."

WITNESS TO A MURDER

*I*n October 1996, I received a several-page, handwritten letter from Lee, an author and retired teacher from South Carolina. Referring to my invitation in the back of *Possessed Possessions* to share unusual tales about other troubled objects, he wrote, "I realized that . . . I had two such pieces, a bed and a dresser, that I came to think of as the Schranck (not the actual name) Murder Dresser. . . . I could empathize with the people in your book who had haunted furniture."

The following story is told through excerpts taken from Lee's detailed letter.

"The dresser never caused me any problem. It caused a nine days' sensation in a small town in western North Carolina, when I taught at a small religious college there a number of years ago."

In the letter, Lee explained that the Schrancks were an German immigrant family that had settled in the area and, for some time, it had been prominent and influential. However, by the days following World War I, only the widow Schranck and her grown son remained.

"He fought in Flanders, was gassed and shell-shocked and came home an invalid," Lee recalled, adding that the mother and son did some farming several miles from town. They lived meagerly until the mother grew very old. The son deteriorated and grew more peculiar.

"Finally, the old lady had a stroke and was left helpless. Neighbors did what they could for her and tried to impress the son that he must care for her as well as he could. He could not understand why she lay in bed and did not cook as she always had done, and at last came to resent her as a burden and killed her with an ax, chopping her head off and cutting her to pieces.

"It was a sensational murder. My landlord had known the Schrancks for generations and may have been distantly related, so I heard more about the murder than had been printed in the papers.

"The son was confined in a mental institution and soon died. The legal heirs, on the West Coast, empowered an attorney to sell the Schranck land and the contents of the house and outbuildings. Most of the furniture was bought by the owner of an antiques and used furniture store.

"Advertised as the Schranck furniture, the collection had great morbid interest, and the murder bed sold immediately at much more than its intrinsic value, though it was a handsome walnut bed, with cannonball finials and fine carvings. . . . I liked the dresser used in the same room, but it also was overpriced, so I shrugged it off.

"A few days went by, then my class in European history met in chaos. The students were so excited about something that I could not quiet them down. I heard a football player say, 'Shut up! I was there. I saw it. I can tell you what happened!'

"I pounded the desk and told the class to listen. He then said, 'I went downtown for lunch, and went in to see that junk from the Schranck auction. Just as I went in, a woman looked at the dresser, screamed and fainted. I rushed to see if I could help her, and saw what caused her to faint. The mirror was showing the old woman being murdered. Just like on a TV screen. It was ghastly!'

"It was my last class of the day, and when it was over I went downtown to see what the store owner would confirm of the wild story. I found the dresser out on the sidewalk. When I asked the proprietor what really had happened, he said, 'Hell! That woman let out a yell you could'a heard up at the college and swooned to the floor. And when I ran to see what was wrong, that crazy fool was choppin' the old woman up. It like to have made me throw up, all that blood and her with her head cut off, right there in the lookin' glass—in that cloudy oldtime mirror, I mean.'

" 'I saw the dresser out on the sidewalk,' I said.

" 'I ain't gonna have it in here,' he said. 'It'll set out there 'til somebody wants it or the trashman picks it up. I wish I'd never heard of that stuff from Schrancks!' "

The dresser had sported a hefty $300 pricetag. But, with very little haggling, Lee secured the attractive piece for the grand sum of $10. He mentioned that he planned to take out the tin mirror and replace it with one made of glass. The dealer suggested that Lee not spend too much money on nice glass. The antique man said he would bet that the scene would return on whatever reflector replaced the original tin piece.

> **❝A woman looked at the dresser, screamed and fainted. The mirror was showing the old woman being murdered. Just like on a TV screen. It was ghastly!❞**

Lee said that the murder scene has never reappeared in the new mirror. He also stripped the dresser's finish and painted floral decorations on its surface, giving it a new appearance. But, none of his children would let him place the piece in their rooms.

". . . and I never have felt comfortable with it or ever near it," he wrote. "It is in a room that I go in as seldom as possible, because every occupant who tried to sleep there declared that it is haunted, and not by a benevolent entity. It is an old house, built in the last century, and the Schranck Murder Dresser seems quite at home there."

CallIng to Me

*I*n the introduction to *Possessed Possessions*, John Sikorski, a Florida antiques dealer and radio show host, commented on antique collectors who have told him that they pass up items because they "didn't speak" to them, while other objects seemed to "call out" for attention.

"Something about it stops you," John said, "and you see it. It's caught your attention. You may even pick it up, and may not be sure as to why."

A few months after the release of *Possessed Possessions*, I received a letter from Jerry Shields, an author who is well known on the Delmarva Peninsula. A former college professor, he writes about literature, history and regional culture—a bit different from my books which focus on folklore, legends and things that go bump in the night.

But, working in the same geographic area, we have run into each other often, exchanged books and spent pleasant sessions sharing leads, discussing mutual acquaintances and talking about books we both would like to complete someday.

It's important to mention that Jerry also is book collector, concentrating on volumes related to English and American literature, Delawareana, American presidents and other particular areas of personal interest.

Jerry's letter, however, mentioned a few personally "rewarding experiences" that he was unable to explain. In each instance, he was "led" to discover items that he found interesting or for which he had been searching.

He described it as similar to dowsing, the art of using a forked wooden tree branch to discover water.

"What I'm describing," he wrote, "is a bit like dowsing, I suppose, except that it involves Delaware items having historic significance and value. Whenever I have this urge, it moves me to go to (or stop at) a certain place, often at a certain time. I never know what I am looking for, but when I find it, I sense that this was the item I came to discover and can stop looking."

In 1994, he made a presentation on "Book Collecting for Fun and Profit: A Love Affair with Books" to the Eastern Shore Writers group in Salisbury, Maryland.

His remarks were fascinating, especially to a collector.

Describing a bibliophile as a person who loves books, Jerry referred to himself as a bibliomane—a shortened version of bibliomaniac—"a person who is crazy about books."

"Where is the line between them?" he asked. "Hard to say, but I know I've crossed it a lot, often to my discomfort but hardly ever to my regret. I suppose it's like the difference between a social drinker and an alcoholic. The bibliomane always finds a good reason for buying a book just as the boozehound justifies drinking."

In the latter portion of his remarks, Jerry said, "But now I'm going to bring up something I almost don't want to talk about, because it's so weird that it has no place at all in my logic. I've tried to dismiss it, but I can't. Nor can I find any acceptable reason as to how or why it happens. I only know it does—very rarely, to be sure—but I speak from personal experience. What I'm telling you is that—once in a great while—books and other inanimate objects seem to *call* me to them!"

His first such experience was while seeking information for a biography of Wilmington, Delaware, writer Christopher Ward. It was one of those ongoing projects that never gets finished, but can't be put away for good.

Normally, on Tuesdays and Fridays, Jerry would go to Spence's Bazaar, an all-day auction and flea market in Dover, not far from his home. His usual custom was to write until noon and head over around lunchtime.

"I don't consider myself to be at all superstitious," he said. "In fact, I'm the least superstitious person I know. But I've also learned to trust my intuition. So, when the urge to go to Spence's early that morning came upon me, I chose to go with it."

Upon arriving, he passed along the first aisle of flea market stalls, stopping at a dealer whose table was piled high with books. Ten seconds later, he spotted a copy of Christopher Ward's first novel, *One Little Man,* published in 1926 and in wonderful condition.

"I had never seen this book before, not even in the libraries where I'd done my research. Yet, here it was, and I could have it for one dollar.

"How did I know it was there? I didn't. When I went down early that morning, I didn't have the vaguest idea of what I was looking for. I only knew that I felt a strong urge to depart from my usual routine and go down then, at that moment. And, for yielding to the urge, I was rewarded in a delightfully unexpected way."

Several months passed before a similar event occurred.

Eventually, something called Jerry to Spence's, and again he passed along the stalls and aisles. This time, however, there was no quick payoff for his efforts. Thinking he would not be rewarded every time, he was ready to leave. But something urged him to stay, to keep looking.

> **66**
> *Why did I go there and keep on looking for some mysterious treasure after my initial search had turned up nothing? I can't tell you, and I can't explain it myself. I just know what I felt.* **99**

Stopping outside, in the area known to display items that are not considered the most desirable offerings at the auction, he came across a box of old books.

"I knelt beside the box, putting my hand on the books to steady myself as I did so. I then looked into the box and saw that my hand was resting on a copy of a book called *Rambles and Reflections* by Thomas J. Clayton."

Recognizing the title and author, Jerry was able to purchase a rare volume that contained a description of life in the early part of the century and a number of Delaware folk stories that had not been available elsewhere.

Obviously satisfied with his finds, he also was a bit concerned.

"The perplexing question remains. Whence came the urge?" he wondered. "Why did I go there and keep on looking for some mysterious treasure after my initial search had turned up nothing? I can't tell you, and I can't explain it myself. I just know what I felt."

Jerry still has no answer for the "little nudges" and "mental urges" that seem to direct him to books and other objects of importance.

But, after having benefited on a few occasions from unexplained, puzzling influences that have led him to personal treasures, he said, "You can believe that the next time I feel an urge, I'm going to do what it tells me."

Bits and Pieces

illy Jo and Bobby lived near Reading, Pennsylvania, and they were in love. Unfortunately, she was 17 and he was 19—too young to be serious about romance and much too young to get married. Also, a few of Bobby's relatives and friends didn't think that Billy Jo came from the right kind of family.

But, young love knows no bounds. Despite warnings and threats from members of both families, the two teenagers continued to see each other and made serious plans to be together forever.

One of the most outspoken critics of their relationship was Bobby's grandmother. Always known to speak her mind and the devil be damned, Grams would "tell it like it is." Plus, it was obvious that the older woman didn't like Billy Jo at all.

After graduating from high school, Bobby joined the Army and was sent overseas. He and Billy Jo broke things off before he left, and everything seemed to settle down for a time.

While he was away, Grams became ill and was staying in the hospital for a few days, undergoing tests.

According to Violet, Bobby's sister, "Grams had been living with us. One night, while she was away and her room was empty, we heard her door open and close, and there was the sound of familiar footsteps coming from down the hall. My mother and I got up to investigate and found that everyone was asleep. But, within minutes the hospital called to say that Grams had passed away."

Bobby was unable to get back for the funeral, but arrived a few weeks later to visit with his family. During his emergency leave, he and Billy Jo got married. When Bobby returned to

Germany, Billy Jo remained behind and stayed with his family—in Grams' room.

"Billy Jo never felt comfortable in that room," Violet said. "She would spend as little time as possible in there. We soon came to realize why Billy Jo felt this way. Even after her death, Grams had not yet vacated her residence."

About two weeks after Billy Jo had moved in, the family was having an informal social hour on the first floor in a room at the opposite end of the house. Suddenly, they all heard crashing and banging coming from the upstairs. Everyone who was in the house at the time went up to investigate with knives in their hands. Slowly, the group went from room to room, peeking and wondering what had happened.

When they entered Grams' former bedroom, they saw the cause of the noise. The deceased's knickknack shelf appeared to have been pulled off the wall and thrown across the room.

"Everything on that shelf, except for one figurine, had been destroyed," Violet recalled. "All of those items had been very special to Grams, and we all were upset about the damage. Even more disturbing was the way the shelf was ripped from the wall. It didn't fall down straight. It was as if someone or something deliberately pulled it out from its holders and threw it across the room."

❝ They saw the cause of the noise. The deceased's knickknack shelf appeared to have been pulled off the wall and thrown across the room. ❞

Terrified from the events, all of the occupants decided to wait at a neighbor's house until Violet's parents came home. In particular, Billy Jo was very upset and after that she spent less time than ever in that room.

"I knew that Grams was not a very forgiving person," Violet said. "I guess Billy Jo also realized that. She also probably figured that if she couldn't win an argument with Grams while she was alive there was no way she was going to win her over after she was dead."

About a month later, Billy Jo joined Bobby in Germany. A few weeks afterwards, Violet and her mother sent the couple a package containing items that Bobby and Billy Jo had requested, plus a few surprise presents.

Among the gifts was the special figurine, the only one that had not been broken when Grams' shelf flew from the wall.

Violet said she was there when her mother wrapped that ceramic item very carefully, surrounding it with paper and towels, and placing it in the very center of the box where it would be safest.

"When the package arrived in Germany," Violet said, "nothing was damaged except for the figurine. It was broken into so many pieces it could never be repaired. Frankly, I think even if it could have been fixed, Billy Jo would not have kept it."

Family Furniture

Maine is a big place. It's especially large when you compare it to a small state like Delaware, where I grew up. You can drive from Delaware's northern border to its southern line in less than two hours. (If you want to travel straight across the second smallest state in the country it takes a lot less time—10 minutes up north, about a good half hour downstate.)

But, Maine!

Up there you are talking about spending some serious traveling time. I drove along its scenic coastal highway, but never got to the top of the state, and I was in the car for almost six hours. I can only imagine how long it would take to travel across Maine—especially since there are few roads that head directly east to west.

When this letter arrived, I was excited and checked out the town of the sender on the Maine state map.

I won't tell you where it is. But I will tell you this: If I put the correct village in this story, everyone in that sleepy little hamlet would know all of the people involved.

We'll just say this story occurred somewhere in the area called Down East, and the names have been changed to hide the identities of the poor souls who were involved in these bizarre events.

The letter read:

"We had received some furniture from my parents. At first, I didn't want to admit it, but wherever there was a piece of furniture from them, things happened.

"We heard voices and noises. My daughter also saw things in her mirror. Also, the furniture affected our personalities. When we gave back the antique furniture, the noises and voices stopped.

"My sister, who kept some of my parents' objects has nothing to do with us. My parents treat us very badly. I don't know whether it's because of the furniture. There is a lot more to share, but it would take too long to write about.

"P.S. Yes. People will not listen or accept what's true. They think it's you. But when you get rid of the items, the problem stops."
    Sincerely,
    Sandy

A follow-up call to Sandy revealed an interesting story that seems to be caused by several possessed items and a very strained family situation.

"I used to go to yard sales," Sandy told me over the phone, "but not anymore. I used to love to stop by the roadside and shop. But that's all over now—since I had trouble with the furniture. I try not to have anything to do with anything unless it's new."

About three years ago, Sandy, her husband Jack and their two daughters moved back to Maine to be close to their families. Soon after they arrived, Sandy's parents gave her some furniture—mainly a few vanities with mirrors, a tall dresser, a large bedframe, a few night stands and a vanity for the bathroom, with a sink bowl and a pair of matching lights.

Not long after the furniture was moved into Sandy and Jack's home, they began to hear noises.

"Disruptions, odd noises and disturbances went off the scale," she said. "It got to the point that we couldn't seem to live with each other. I never got along with my father. He was demanding and difficult to deal with. So I didn't want anything from him. I felt uncomfortable accepting the furniture right in the beginning. But that angered him so we took it against my better judgment."

Eventually, the sounds of moving furniture began to occur each night. But when Sandy or Jack got up to investigate they couldn't find any logical cause.

One night, checking on her older daughter, Sandy leaned over the teenager's bed and the young girl grabbed her mother by the neck. As the girl pulled her mother down and their faces met, Sandy noticed that the girl's eyes had a reddish glow and were very strange. The next morning, her daughter acted as if nothing had happened.

Sandy decided to keep quiet about the incident, hoping it was a bad dream or that it wouldn't happen again.

In the middle of a subsequent night, Sandy entered her older daughter's room to check on the girl and saw the bed elevating about the floor.

"I told my husband about the incidents, but he didn't want to hear anything about it. He ignored me. I told him maybe the solution was to get rid of the furniture, if we gave things back circumstances might get better. At that time, he didn't want to hear it. It was a small town and people would talk. I guess he figured things would blow over if we waited long enough."

As the noises and strange incidents continued, Sandy's younger daughter started to become afraid to go into the bathroom that the girls shared. That door would shut and open on its own, and there seemed to be something strange about the vanity with the mirror that was placed in the younger girl's bedroom.

A short time later, Sandy's younger daughter mentioned that she had seen a small figure come out of the bathroom, near where the vanity was located. It looked like a woman about 12 inches high and she wore a hat. Sandy's daughter called her the "Little Lady." She said when she turned on the light the strange figure disappeared.

"Unusual things were occurring on a regular basis," Sandy said. "Noises, doors closing, appearances by the 'Little Lady.' But the thing that bothered me most was the effect all this was having on our personalities. We weren't ourselves any longer. We were arguing, or we were distant. I was afraid for my daughters and myself, for my whole family."

One weekend, when Jack was away, the older daughter came home from school in an hysterical state. She was irrational, not the same person, Sandy said, recalling the incident. "We were all screaming and yelling. It was horrible."

When Sandy went upstairs to check on her daughter, she found the girl in the bathroom ready to swallow a handful of pills.

"I put everyone in the car and we went to church to pray," Sandy said. "I knew we were in trouble. When we all went to bed that night, I slept downstairs. I knew the furniture had to go.

"The next day, we got up and left the house, spent the day walking and in restaurants. We talked a lot. My daughters said they saw things in the mirrors. They felt something was in the room with them, that they were never alone. They felt they were being watched all the time."

The women got through the weekend alone, but it was very difficult. When Sandy told Jack what had occurred, he said, very calmly, "When you decide to get rid of the furniture, this will all stop."

Together they loaded the dressers and vanities—plus the bed frame that they had never erected—into a truck and dropped it all off on Sandy's parents lawn.

"When my father gave us the furniture," she said, "he made the stipulation that if we ever didn't keep it we had to give it back to him. Even though we got rid of it, I am scared to death of him to this day. I called my mother 10 times to explain why I sent it back, but she didn't want to hear it. I know I did the right thing. I couldn't help it. I was dealing with my daughter's life."

Later, Sandy went through the house and gathered up everything else she had ever received from her parents—jewelry, dishes, any type of gift. She stored it all in a box in her shed and eventually sold it off.

❝I felt uncomfortable accepting the furniture right in the beginning. But that angered him so we took it against my better judgment.❞

When Sandy called her sister to explain the situation, a fight occurred. Since then, they have only talked to each other once in nearly four years.

Sandy has tried to figure out the puzzle and determine some explanation for her horrifying experiences. To do this, she has recalled some of the strange incidents that happened while she was growing up.

"My sister and I used to sit in the attic and hear evil laughter," Sandy said. "We would tell our father and mother, but they would say it was the ducks quacking or offer some other excuse. I also recall seeing strange faces in the windows. My father was very bad. He would beat us to a pulp, until we were black and blue. But when we were bleeding, he told us he did it because he loved us."

But the causes for the unusual events apparently go beyond one generation.

Sandy said her mother used to tell her stories.

"She told me that her mother, my grandmother, used to tell her about a young girl who looked in the mirror, while she was combing her hair, and a creature came out through the glass and clawed her to death. I thought she was kidding. But to this day, my mother doesn't spend any time in front of a mirror.

"She also told me how her mother's mother, my great-grandmother, talked to Satan and once she was so upset that she caused a wall to collapse. All this bothered me. That's part of why I didn't feel it was safe to have their furniture."

When Sandy and Jack shared their thoughts about the ordeal with the local minister he, as Sandy explained, "treated us like we had the plague. Nobody seemed to acknowledge that my father and mother could be wrong. Everyone thought they were the pride of the community. Only one elderly friend knew my father was very evil, but no one else."

Sandy said she believes the proof of her concerns was demonstrated in the improved mood of her children and the calm atmosphere in her home.

"The change was very fast, almost immediate," she said. "My daughter's disposition changed for the better. There was a different atmosphere in the house. Some of our friends told us later that they could sense the improvement.

"We don't buy any antiques. If it's new, I can sleep; and I don't have to worry about it at all. If I went to a yard sale, I'd have to wonder who owned it, if it ever caused a problem and I don't want to deal with that ever again.

"I know other people have experienced worse things that we have. But I never imagined that objects could cause you to become so depressed that you couldn't handle emotional problems. And when we told people about what was happening and they said we weren't telling the truth, we were crushed."

Bed from Beyond

*M*arie lives on Long Island, New York, and she has had more than her share of paranormal experiences. We began corresponding in the spring of 1996. Since then, through several letters and a few phone conversations, she has been kind enough to describe her participation in unusual events that have included spectral sightings, psychic dreams, moving objects and being touched by unseen phantoms.

By far, however, her most interesting story involves her haunted bed.

In the early 1980s, during a trip to visit friends in upstate New York, she passed through a mall and noticed a most unusual waterbed.

"I fell in love with 'The Bed,' " Marie said. "It was a lush, mahogany-stained, wooden poster bed. It had a frame with drawers in it, wooden columns and a huge wooden headboard that supported a 'ceiling' of etched mirrors. The headboard had a huge matching etched mirror, two glass-doored cabinets, curved shelves and two lighted sconces.

"It was the most Victorian-looking modern bed I had ever seen. With the dim light in the store and the red satin sheets, the bed was absolutely breathtaking. I said to my friend, 'When I get married someday, I'm buying that bed.' "

A few years later, Marie told her fiance about her special bed. They drove upstate and it, or another model, was still available. They purchased it with some loan money and they were very excited when it arrived and was erected in their new apartment.

Marie told me that up to that point she was happy and content. Her life wasn't perfect, but neither was it chaotic. She liked her job, there were no major catastrophes and the future was promising.

When she met her fiance, Ron, their personalities matched, and a brief and wonderful courtship led to a fantastic wedding.

"We went to our apartment," she said. "The landlords loved us, and it was only a few blocks from my parents' house. Money was tight, and most of our things were donated by relatives. With both of us working full time, we were only able to pay the rent and buy our food. But, we were very happy and we adored each other."

Reflecting on all that has occurred, Marie said her calm world seemed to change overnight after the arrival of The Bed.

"Things have changed, and they have never been the same," she said. "The minute Ron finished putting up the bed, I sensed a change of atmosphere in the apartment. We suddenly, unexplainably, began having violent arguments. We had never argued before."

> **"** *The minute Ron finished putting up the bed, I sensed a change of atmosphere in the apartment. We suddenly, unexplainably, began having violent arguments.* **"**

The day Ron was filling the waterbed mattress up with water, the landlord came by. When she found out about the waterbed she told the newlyweds to get rid of "that thing" or move out.

The problem was settled when Ron threw out the waterbed mattress and instead filled the huge Victorian bed frame with two regular mattresses.

One day after work, while resting on the bed, Marie looked up at one of the dark corner posts and noticed a face-like figure, peeking at her from behind the tall post. During the next few days, Ron saw dark floating forms passing along the hallway.

"The atmosphere in the entire apartment was very heavy and oppressive," Marie said. "We both connected it to The Bed, but I wasn't about to give it up."

The landlord continued to hassle them and they continued to argue between themselves.

During a week-long vacation away from the area, they had a wonderful time and they believed they were totally back on track—until they arrived home.

"The morning after our return to the apartment," Marie said, "we had such a terrible fight. Ron threatened to move out or drop me off at my parents' home. In the next few weeks, he started having 'night terrors.' He would jump up from sleeping, grab his pillow for protection and scream. And this went on night after night. Sometimes, he would throw pillows at a 'demon' that he saw in the corner of the room."

Over the next few years, Marie and Ron moved frequently. Sometimes they lived in apartments. During other times they stayed with relatives. But things never worked out and they and their bed were forced to relocate.

Marie lost her job.

Her father became very ill and died.

Ron lost his job.

They could never get along with their neighbors.

Marie became so sick that she could not get another job and could not eat. Her mother was stricken with a serious disease.

"So that is where I stand now," Marie said. "I still live at my mom's house. She's still very ill. My physical condition has not improved. And my relationship with my husband has never been able to get back to the wonderful way it was in the beginning.

"Have the past dozen years just been a string of bad luck," Marie asked, "or does The Bed have something to do with it? I know you're probably saying, 'There's only one way to find out.' But what if I got rid of The Bed and nothing improved? I still love that bed. I could never get rid of it until I could replace it with something more beautiful, which would be hard to find.

"Have you ever heard of anything like this happening to anyone else?"

Pirate Treasure

rom the late 1600s until about 1750, scores of pirates roamed the seas off the East Coast of the new American continent. These thieves—also known as picaroons and buccaneers—attacked civilian and military ships on the high seas, stealing all they could haul away and often sinking the ships and killing the passengers and crew.

When the buccaneers needed supplies, they headed for land. Small seaside villages on the coasts of Delaware, Maryland and New Jersey were regular stops for the thieves of the sea.

According to a well-known and often repeated legend, pirate leaders—including Edward "Blackbeard" Teach and Captain William Kidd—would take several crew members ashore to bury chests filled with stolen goods. Tales still abound of large wooden boxes overflowing with gold coins, silver bars and dazzling jewelry that are waiting to be discovered.

But, the legends also state that with each precious fortune hidden ashore, pirate leaders would leave one crew member behind to guard the gold for all eternity. Usually the captain murdered an unsuspecting sailor after the hole had been dug, and the dead crewman's body was tossed atop the treasure chest. It's believed that bad luck and ill health will haunt anyone who seeks to take away the buried gold and dares to disturb the resting place of the cursed pirate skeleton.

For hundreds of years, modern day treasure hunters have employed sophisticated, high-tech equipment—including satellite imagery—to try to locate and secure these long lost treasures. But, to date, no one has reported locating the hidden loot. Others say some of the riches have been found, but the lucky prospectors have not admitted their good luck and kept details about the location and the value of the find to themselves.

Who could blame them?

Perhaps they believe there is more treasure nearby. Maybe they couldn't haul it all away, and they go back periodically to secure more of Blackbeard's bountiful booty.

And some say they know exactly where the treasure is located, but they are too afraid to return and claim their share.

I was told this story by an old man in Delaware City, Delaware. The old seaport town has seen better days. Today, only a few commercial fishermen remain. Most have passed onto their eternal reward and others have given up the sea and taken jobs that offer steady employment, more money and a high degree of boredom and dissatisfaction.

On the weekends, the few remaining frustrated sailors head out into the Delaware River and Bay, to see what they can catch and, for a short time, they are back at the helm, smelling the sea air and doing what they enjoy most.

It was in the early evening, in late October, when I met Rob at the Canal Inn. The well-known watering hole stands at the edge of Clinton Street in downtown D.C. (Delaware City), overlooking the black water of the Delaware River.

He was a few years shy of 60, with a pot belly and a full gray beard. White hair sprouted from both sides of his battered and stained, red Phillies cap. His voice was raspy and low, but he talked quickly. His dark eyes darted continually from side to side, as if trying to catch anyone who might be attempting to listen in on our conversation.

A mutual friend had arranged the meeting. I never got Rob's last name, and I never saw him again. But I recall the story he told, and I believed everything he said.

He started his tale by talking about Fort Delaware, a pentagon-shaped, granite-walled Civil War fort located on Pea Patch Island in the middle of the Delaware River.

The structure was completed in 1860. Originally, it was built as a coastal fortification to stop Confederate gunboats from attacking Philadelphia and other towns along the busy East Coast waterway. However, by 1862, Confederate prisoners started arriving; and, for the remaining years of the War Between the States, Fort Delaware and the rest of Pea Patch Island became a prison camp for Confederate soldiers.

Eventually, nearly 33,000 Rebels would live on the island. Slightly more than 2,400 would die and be buried at Finns Point, across the river in New Jersey. Not too many would escape. The river and its swift current made sure of that.

Some believe the ghosts of these dead prisoners roam the corridors of Fort Delaware, and there have been a number of sightings. In fact, each summer park historians relate the fort's history and I share its ghost stories as we jointly conduct Ghost/Lantern Tours on the island.

"I went over to the island real late one night," Rob said, whispering and looking around the room. "The fort was locked up. They do that, you know. Shut up the big heavy metal doors. You can't get in. And I'm not going to go across that moat. No way!"

"Why?" I asked.

"Hell! They got hungry muskrats and real rats and who knows what else down in there. Probably quicksand. Suck you right down quick. So, anyway, I started checking out the island. I got a pretty good detector, and I set it so to pick up coins on the meter."

I interrupted him a moment and asked, "Isn't that against the law? I thought you couldn't metal detect on state property."

Rob shook his head in disgust. "Hell, where you comin' from, man? You born this mornin'? That's why I went on over at night. Tied up my boat. Not likely that no water ranger is gonna come over very often. He's got more important things to do than check out the island in the middle of the night. I was playing the odds that nobody would go by and see my boat and call it in. So I took the chance, 'cause I figured it was worth it, 'specially if I found the big find." Then he looked at me and laughed. "Hah! You got to pay to play! Right?"

I nodded and waited. He continued.

"Now. Here's the good part. The reason I ain't never goin' back over there again. I'm working the big open field in front of the fort real good, see? Getting' some little blips on the screen, but nothin' big. Then, I start to move north, up toward where the big birds live. In that sanctuary, they call it.

"That's when I see a glow in the high reeds, like a big movin' light bulb the size of a deer. Hell, half scared me to death, I tell ya. But I went to see what it was all about. It was going down the trail real fast and I had to run to catch up."

Rob explained that every time he got close enough to get a good look, the glow moved abruptly to the left or right and gained speed, as if it were playing with him.

"I was gettin' pissed off," he said, shaking his head. "And I was just about ready to leave, when the thing stopped dead—about 30 feet in front of me. I stood still, sort of waitin' it out. Then, after about two minutes, I picked up my detector and started walkin' toward it, real slow, tryin' not to make no noise.

"I got within' five feet and stopped, and there was a smell that hit me. I tell ya, it was horrible—like a dead animal or skunk. As I went to pull my shirt up and put it over my nose and mouth, this long arm comes outta the glow and points at the ground.

> **❝ I used my free hand to grab my metal detector and swing it across and smash the skeleton hand to hell. ❞**

"Hell! I'm gettin' sick from the smell, the bright yellow light is hurtin' my eyes, but I get the feelin' this thing is trying to tell me where to look. I figure gold or treasure or some kinda fortune is down there. Then, like a flash, the gold glow disappears and I'm standin' in the dark all alone."

As Rob took a sip of his beer, I asked, "What did you do then?"

"I didn't waste no time at all. I turned on that machine and put it right over the spot that the glowin' thing pointed at."

"And?"

"And she went off the mark. Hell, I tell ya, my needle jumped to the other end of the meter. And I said, 'This is it, mamma!' "

Rob said that for a half hour he dug with his entrenching tool until he had a hole about two feet deep. Just as he was about to stop, he heard metal scrapping against the tip of his shovel.

"I got real excited! Damn! My ship done come in. I knew it. I bent real low and was diggin' real fast. No tellin' how long before the cops might come by, or daylight would start to come up. So I had to move fast. After about a half hour, 45 minutes at the most, I had cleared off a good section, and I could tell that I was lookin' at the top of a wooden chest.

"Now, they say Blackbeard and Captain Kidd and them other pirates buried treasure up and down the coast. But nobody never thought they would go onto Pea Patch and hide their loot. That's what I figured, anyway. So, I just happened to be in the right place at the right time.

"Just as I was diggin' around the front of the chest, to get to the lid opening, that's when all hell broke loose."

"What do you mean?" I asked.

"Well, let me tell you this, first. I don't give a damn if you believe me or not, but what I'm tellin' ya really is true. It may sound like I been snortin' mushrooms or smokin' grass or hittin' the sauce, but I'm tellin' ya what happened. On my holy dead mother's grave, I swear it all. Understand?"

I nodded.

He continued. "As I'm fumblin' with the lid, tryin' to pull it up, this hand. A white skeleton hand, with bone fingers, comes up from the underside of the chest and grabs my wrist. I tell ya, it's like a vise. It was real tight, and it starts pullin' me down onto the top of the chest. I swear, I was givin' it all the strength I got to pull away, and I can't stop it. I'm too scared or able to shout for help.

"My mind is flashin' with pictures of pirates and dead men on the top of the treasure box—like they used to talk about— and I swear to God if He let's me outta this mess I'll mend my thievin' ways.

"As I'm pullin', and it's no use, I used my free hand to grab my metal detector and swing it across and smash the skeleton hand to hell. I mean, I beat the crap outta that monster. When it let go, I was up on my feet and runnin' hell bent for leather outta that trail with my metal detector in hand.

"I never looked back. I never went back. I never wanna go back. They can have their damn treasure and the island, too. I want no part of it. No way!"

He was done. Sweat had appeared on his forehead, and as he raised his voice a few others in the bar had turned their head to listen.

Another old drunk, they figured, as they shook their heads and returned to their business.

But I knew better. I believed him.

"I was this close," he said, spreading his fingers an inch apart and holding them in front of my eyes. "If I coulda held on and got into that box, I wouldn't be here talkin' to you right now. No, sir! I'd be on some tropical island, drinkin' and havin' native girls keepin' me cool with big feathered fans. But, that's life."

"What do you think it was?" I asked.

"Hell! It was the treasure guard, of course. They say they left a dead pirate behind to guard their gold. The way I see it, this one's persistent, and he's still at it—and doin' a good job, too."

"You're sure you won't go back?"

"No way! You think I'm nuts? I gotta few good years left, and I ain't gonna cut 'em short for no lost treasure. They almost got me, but not quite. I got away once. I ain't gonna give 'em another chance."

"But you really think there's treasure on the island?"

"I know there's treasure on that island. But, it's cursed for sure. And it ain't worth dyin' over. Not for me, anyway."

Knickknacks

Feeling Cross

*J*ennifer wrote to share a story that happened in Brooklyn, New York, several years ago when she was 13 years old.

At the time, her mother's boyfriend had stopped by the apartment to visit and noticed a brown paper bag—the kind people get at supermarkets—sitting in a corner in the building's first-floor hallway.

The man picked it up and took it inside Jennifer's apartment. After resting it on the table, he pulled out a variety of strange looking statues and odd-shaped, colored cloths with ornate designs.

"We took notice of a cross that was inside the bag," Jennifer recalled. "It was covered in black and was supported on a small wooden block. It was made of strange material, and it looked like it would glow in the dark."

Jennifer remembered that her grandmother had always said that whenever you found a cross you should never bring it into your house until it was blessed.

"At the time I knew I shouldn't touch it or any of the things in the bag," Jennifer said. "They didn't belong to us, and I felt strange about the mysterious bag." She looked at the objects and wondered:

Who did they belong to?

Where did they come from?

Despite these concerns, Jennifer took the smooth cross and went inside one of the apartment closets, to see if it would glow in the dark.

"As soon as I closed the door," she said, "I looked at the outline of the cross in the darkness and it started glowing this ugly green color. Then I started to hear evil, church-like music, or maybe it was some kind of evil chanting. I also felt negative energy coming from the cross, and I had an overwhelming feeling that something definitely was not right with the cross."

She ran out of the closet and told her mother what she had experienced. Jennifer also said she immediately suggested that they get rid of the cross. While her mother did not believe the entire story, she did agree to dispose of the mysterious cross.

"To this day," Jennifer said, "I will never forget the feeling I felt when I saw that cross glow green and that horrible music played in my mind."

"It's mine, fool!"

A collector of Civil War memorabilia had made it his goal to locate all of the equipment and uniform pieces of a particular Union officer. After many years of searching antique shops, tables at re-enactments, mail order catalogs and advertisements in Civil War oriented publications, the searcher needed only one item, the officer's military cap to complete his collection.

One weekend, while browsing through a shop that specialized in old military uniforms, the collector came upon a piece of headgear that fit the bill. Its style, color and condition—plus the shop owner's comments regarding the cap's authenticity—allowed the collector to believe that this was, indeed, the exact uniform cap for which he had been searching for so long.

After purchasing the headgear, he carefully placed his new found treasure on the passenger seat of his car and headed for home. In a few short hours, the short-brimmed cap would take its place with the rest of the deceased Civil War Union officer's uniform.

But, the longer the man drove, the more his doubts increased. As time passed, the more skeptical he became. Eventually, his excitement had evaporated, and a sense of dejection had replaced the initial enthusiasm that had accompanied his find.

As the unaccompanied driver pulled away from a stop light, and at that moment not in the best frame of mind, he heard a strange voice announce: "It's mine, fool!"

The sound came from the passenger's seat—vacant except for the 135-year-old military cap that was heading home to be reunited with the rest of the deceased soldier's uniform.

Tick Tock

On several occasions I have been told stories about clocks that have stopped at the time of a person's death. Usually, this happens to a timepiece that is located in the room of the deceased. In most of the stories, at some point in time after the ceremonies or burial, someone will notice that a clock in the home is stuck— or stopped running—at the time of the recent death.

Fewer instances have been reported of broken clocks beginning to work again after someone has died. But, in one highly unusual case, a large grandfather clock—that stood in the downstairs hallway and had been jammed or broken for years—suddenly began to chime only moments after the owner of the home had died in his second-floor bedroom.

Sights and Sounds

•My friend Ted, from Wilmington, Delaware, found a picture of an interesting lighthouse in a book he borrowed from the library. A creative fellow and a local folk artist, he built a replica of that lighthouse out of wood and placed it in his backyard.

Later, he read that there was a ghost story associated with that East Coast beacon. The isolated outpost was said to be haunted by the "Lady in White."

Not long after his model was completed, Brynn, Ted's grand-daughter—who knew nothing of the legend of the haunted lady—looked out his kitchen window and announced, "Grandpa! There's a lady in white going from your lighthouse into your shed!"

Ted ran to the window and saw nothing. He also checked the shed, and it was empty. He found no visitor, spirited or earthly.

But, just what did Ted's young granddaughter see?

• Talk about strange sights. There is no tale of haunting related to this report, but it is worth sharing.

An East Coast real estate agent was showing a client around town. As they passed an attractive home in a nice neighborhood with a sale sign on the lawn, the customer asked why the agent wasn't stopping at that particular home.

"I don't think it's right for you," she replied.

"Why not?" the customer said. "It looks fine to me. What could possibly be wrong with it?"

The agent calmly explained, "The former owner used actual tombstones for the base of the backyard patio. It's an interesting and one-of-a-kind feature, but that's not the kind of extra that makes a house easy to sell."

The client agreed. They found something a bit more suitable.

• Deborah, a friend of mine in Pennsylvania, is a well-known area storyteller. Deborah interviewed an elderly woman about an ancestor who was a general in the Civil War. Deborah taped the conversation, which was conducted in an old home beneath a large portrait of the general.

The elderly woman described incidents that occurred during a battle that her relative had been in, and she also discussed stories about customs and life during earlier periods in American history.

Some time later, when Deborah played back the interview, she said she heard musket fire coming from the tape. Of course, there were no such sounds during the interview.

No one can explain how the crackle of gunfire and bursts of cannon materialized.

•In Washington, D.C., an antique typewriter—which has no ribbon or paper and is used only as a showpiece—is believed to operate on its own.

The owner reported that on several occasions he has heard the keys strike and the bell ring, indicating the carriage has reached its limit, at odd hours of the morning.

He said he was thinking of installing a new ribbon and placing a blank piece of paper in the machine, to see what important message the spirit is trying to send from the Great Beyond.

Ouija Board

Nancy, a Pennsylvania college student, and three friends were playing with her Ouija board. Almost immediately, they were able to contact a roving spirit who helped them spell out his name—"Nevin."

But he apparently wasn't in heaven.

"He wrote that he could see us through a candle," said Nancy. "Nevin said it was a type of portal to the other side. He also said he didn't like all of us and he had us spell out the word 'suicide.' "

Afraid and upset, they put the board away, but that didn't help.

Within a 10 days, Nancy's car had two flat tires and four lug nuts fell off one of her wheels. One of her roommates got a flat tire. While riding with one of her roommates, the car radio went off and then came back on. But it changed stations on its own.

"It was playing 'The Devil Went Down to Georgia.' We never listen to country," Nancy said. "It was really strange. Because of the car problems and other things, I became terrified and thought it was trying to kill me or one of us. We pulled out the board and asked Nevin if he did the bad things. He said, 'Yes!' We really freaked then, and we put the board away for good.

"At 2 in the morning, when I was home alone, a large porcelain clown flew off the windowsill. It stopped and then started to roll again. There was no way it could have done it on its own. It had to be pushed or rolled by someone. I really lost it then. One of our roommates moved out. Things were getting bizarre. We heard growling sounds coming from outside the window where the clown fell from. It sounded like a werewolf. It was evil. Then there was nasty laughter."

A few months later, when the group's lease was up, only one of the four girls stayed in the apartment. All the other three—including Nancy—moved away.

They keep in touch, but they don't talk about the Ouija board or mention the name Nevin.

"I still get upset whenever I hear 'The Devil Went Down to Georgia,' " Nancy said.

Fertile Minds

An East Coast art gallery has a large number of African masks in its permanent collection. During one particular year, an unusually large number of women working at the museum became pregnant.

The coincidence became a well-known joke among the employees. Several suggested that it was probably caused by the water.

That seemed as good an explanation as any, until it was discovered that the frequently displayed and often cleaned—and touched—pieces of authentic African folk art were fertility masks.

Tuck Me In

In northern Oregon, a man bought a Renaissance revival bed that he estimated was built in the 1870s in the Midwest. He said he found it partially hidden in the back of a shop and was able to secure it for an "incredibly cheap price."

He described it as being solidly made. The headboard was about seven foot high and almost as long, with a lot of decorative carvings of urns and flowers and all sorts of other ornate engravings.

One evening, after erecting the structure, he awoke in the middle of the night with a chill. Before he could grab for a blanket that was folded at the foot of the bed, a man—in Victorian style clothing only visible from the waist up—floated near the bedside and lifted the blanket up to the sleepy man's neck.

"I wasn't sure if I was dreaming or if it really happened," the man told me. "But, I continued to use the bed. I also believed that the spirit had shown up because I was cold. I was very sure to be warm after that night. I thought that if I were cold again he might come back."

Admitting that the story is a bit bizarre, the gentleman added that he sold the bed at a garage sale in Oregon and never heard anything more about it again.

Dolls with an Attitude

Many reports of strange incidents have been associated with dolls, and not just old antiques. Modern looking, plastic creatures also seem to exhibit spirited activity.

•A Pennsylvania shop owner said he believes an imported English doll, that had been used by vaudeville performers just after the turn of the century, is responsible for strange happenings in his shop.

• A doll collector in one unspecified Southern town keeps her precious ceramic figurines locked inside an antique, glass-fronted cabinet. Unfortunately, about once a year something occurs that makes the glass windows break. But, the cause is from the "inside" of the locked cabinet, since shards and broken particles are found on the carpet in front of the handsome piece of furniture.

One neighbor suggested that the dolls are fighting and not getting along. Perhaps they can't handle being cooped up together for so long.

• A Virginia teenager and his friends are so annoyed (and afraid) of his mother's doll collection that they throw stones and pieces of food at the eerie stuffed figures that are lined up in the hallway leading to his mother's bedroom.

• A Maryland antique dealer has been annoyed by a teddy bear that seems to crave attention. The bear is perched on top of a large wardrobe. On one occasion, the gentleman was reading in bed and noticed dust being blown or tossed from the top of the cabinet.

He looked up to see minute dust particles reflected in the light as they fell from the flat surface of the furniture toward the room's hardwood floor.

The only thing nearby was the old, brown, stuffed bear.

• A homeowner in Connecticut moved into a farmhouse he had purchased from an older couple who left to retire in Florida. To ease their move, the former owners had left a fair amount of furniture and assorted household items.

In the second-floor master bedroom, a large doll house stood in the middle of the floor. One of the first things the new resident did was push the four-foot-tall, Victorian-style structure against the wall. That evening, he experienced a life-like dream. In it a little girl was crying in the center of the room.

During the rest of the week, the dream was repeated each night, and every time it was exactly the same: A small, blond-headed child, clothed in a white cotton nightgown and wearing no shoes, stood in the center of the room and cried.

One night, unable to sleep, the man sat up in bed reading. At 3 o'clock in the morning, he noticed movement at the foot of his bed and he saw the young girl materialize in front of his awestruck eyes. Then, knowing she had his attention, she made no sound but pointed to the doll house and disappeared.

The man thought for some time about the significance of the scene. The next morning, he examined the doll house. After a few moments, he noticed that the open end—where children play with the structure—was pushed against the wall. Deciding the child could not get to her play area, the man returned the building to the center of the room to allow the young ghost maximum accessibility.

That night he slept until morning. When he awoke the doll house appeared to be undisturbed.

Naturally, the structure remains in the center of the room to this very day. But, he has moved his bed to another room on the second floor.

No Hands

A young couple moved into a home in a quiet New Jersey suburb. The previous owners had left a lot of junk in the garage. A few weeks after they moved in, the couple decided it was finally time to attack the garage and sort out the good from the bad.

Several hours passed and they had divided the material into two lots—a keep section and a throw away pile.

While taking a short break and sitting on the ground, they heard a sound. Turning in unison, they both saw a two-wheeled bicycle—that had been near the pile of articles to be junked—moving in a circle. As they watched in disbelief, the riderless bike made two small smooth circles in front of the garage and stopped in front of the pile of items to be saved.

As the rusted and dented bike fell against the ground, the husband said, "I guess this means it stays."

What's in a Picture?

Amber from Vestal, New York, sent me a letter describing incidents relating to her painting "Girl With Fruit," which she found in a local antique shop.

She also sent me a picture of the artwork. In the color photograph, a thick, ornate, gold frame surrounds a blond-headed girl who is seated and holding a wooden bowl filled with fruit.

"One night, I awoke around 3 a.m.," Amber said, "and I glanced at the picture. I was amazed to see the girl's hands picking up the fruit and moving it around. A night light in the adjacent bathroom throws just enough light to the hallway to make this painting clearly visible."

But, the woman added, that was only the beginning. More strange episodes were to follow.

"Sometimes," Amber said, "a black cloud floats in front of the picture. Once it floated over to the door of my bedroom, paused and then floated away. Another time, there were hands on the girl's wrist that looked like they were trying to pick her up out of the frame. Also, once it looked like she was trying to climb out of the frame."

Amber admitted she is the only one who has witnessed these "apparitions," and her family and friends tend to humor her and suggest that she has been dreaming.

"But," Amber added, "they do admit the girl's eyes follow them when they move down the hallway. And they've also seen that the frame is tilted in the mornings, although I straightened it the night before. But, it doesn't matter what anyone thinks. I know what I've seen."

Solving the Problem

I received a copy of a newspaper article in the mail. Although I cannot identify the publication, the story indicated that a family had bought a set of bunk beds. Eventually, they decided that the beds were haunted and were nothing but trouble.

Rather than give them away and pass the evil spirits on, they solved the problem by burying the possessed furniture in their own backyard.

Problem solved, until they or the next owners decide to put in a pool.

Good Advice

After a storytelling program in Baltimore, a young man named Jerry asked if I would speak to him for a few minutes about a strange situation.

Thinking there isn't much I haven't heard, I prepared for a story of late night footsteps, active doors, mysterious voices or tales about the smell of cigar smoke in a non-smoking house.

I was totally wrong.

"I want to talk to you about my uncle," he said.

"What about him?" I asked.

"Have you ever heard of people coming back and living in your flower bed or vegetable garden?"

"That's a new one," I said, totally surprised but eager to hear more.

Jerry explained that Uncle El seemed to communicate through the vegetables and plants. Every now and then, Uncle El will send a message when Jerry is picking a tomato off the vine or uprooting a ripe carrot.

"What does he say?" I wondered aloud.

"Not much. Sometimes he tells me not to water 'cause it's going to rain soon."

"Is he right?"

"Most of the time. I got to the point that I listen to him now. In the beginning I ignored the voices. Thought I was crazy. But not anymore."

I assured Jerry that listening to Uncle El was the right thing to do.

He didn't have anything else to share and neither did I.

Masonic Ring

A friend of mine named Billie, from the Western Shore of Maryland, shared a story with me about her uncle's Masonic stick-pin, a ceremonial piece of jewelry some men wear in their lapels.

Billie was given the piece after her uncle's death. She took it to a Baltimore jeweler to have the pin's diamond and seal removed, and turned into a pinkie ring for her.

"I felt it would keep my uncle close to me," she said, "but perhaps the idea of a Catholic or anyone other than a Mason wearing the emblem wasn't too smart."

Absolutely delighted with the results, Billie began wearing the ring immediately.

"But, on the third day," she said, pausing to add, "have you ever noticed that 'things' come in threes? Anyway, on the third day, a deep red circle—like a cigarette burn—appeared on my little finger."

The back of the ring was solid, and it was a comfortable fit, she explained, but to try to solve the problem she put the ring away for a few days. After a full week, the red mark on her finger began to fade.

Happy that the problem was resolved, Billie put the ring on again. But, on the third day, just like before, the ugly red spot returned.

"It didn't itch or burn, nor was there any type of irritation to the touch. And there was no swelling of any kind."

After taking the ring off a second time, Billie returned to the jeweler to inquire about the source of the pinkie ring that he had used. She was informed that no one had worn it before.

The materials in that lot were from new stock that had just arrived. He assured her of the quality of the ring, it was an excellent grade of gold.

"I thanked him and then came home to ponder the Masonic background of the seal. As much as I regretted it," Billie said, "I never wore the ring again.

"Do you believe the ring is evil?" Billie asked me.

I didn't offer an answer.

"I just can't believe such to be the case. But," she concluded, "perhaps if you aren't a Mason, you shouldn't wear a Masonic seal."

Haunted Hearse

In Harrington, Delaware, a black, horsedrawn hearse from the last century stands in the display room of an interesting museum operated by the Harrington Historical Society. The death wagon is a remarkable piece of fine, old-time craftsmanship sporting polished wood, large-spoked wheels and silver accented filigree. Clear glass windows line the sides and rear, so you are able to see the coffin as it passes by at the front of the procession.

A folktale was told to me one evening when I was in the museum. The teller couldn't verify it as true, but it's certainly worth sharing.

The story goes that a young boy went inside the hearse to play. After shutting the rear door, he was scampering around having a gay old time.

Inside, at the bottom of the coffin-holding area, are rollers that are useful when the pallbearers slide the casket in and out of the hearse. Suddenly, people in the museum heard the boy in the hearse crying and carrying on and banging on the glass.

When they opened the back door and let him out, the frightened tot said the rollers started up on their own and were spinning fast, as if someone was pushing them.

Maybe the boy happened to hit them accidentally, with his foot or shoulder or knee. If so, the unexpected spinning startled him and the sight and sound scared him half to death. But what if the hallowed chamber—that has hauled so many corpses to their final resting place—did not want to be used as a playpen?

It would be natural for the phantom of the hearse to use the rollers to signal, very definitely, that playtime was over.

Two for the Road

Two collectors I met in the research for this book stand out as the most unusual—not because of any experiences they shared, but because of the items they enjoy finding.

• A former resident of the East Coast who now lives in the foothills of the Appalachians collects old military weapons, including muskets, rifles, knives and swords. But, his most prized possessions are those that have what appears to be blood remnants on the grips or blades.

He told me, "I keep those in the most temperature controlled environment. And I'm very careful with the swords when I remove them from their scabbard. I don't want to mar the blood-stains that have been there for so long."

• A New Jersey man collects Nazi memorabilia from the World War II era. One evening he sat displaying a few rings and pins with skull-and-crossbones insignia.

Proudly holding a ring up in the air, he said, "Imagine, this piece used to be the personal ring of one of Hitler's most trusted generals, and now it's mine."

Imagine that!

About the Author

*E*d Okonowicz, a Delaware native and freelance writer, is an editor and writer at the University of Delaware, where he earned a bachelor's degree in music education and a master's degree in communication.

Also a professional storyteller, Ed is a member of the National Storytelling Association. He presents programs at country inns, retirement homes, schools, libraries, private gatherings, public events, Elderhostels and theaters in the mid-Atlantic region.

He specializes in local legends and folklore of the Delaware and Chesapeake Bays, as well as topics related to the Eastern Shore of Maryland. He also writes and tells city stories, many based on his youth growing up in his family's beer garden–Adolph's Cafe–in the Browntown section of Wilmington, Delaware.

Ed presents storytelling courses and writing workshops based on his book *How to Conduct an Interview and Write an Original Story*. With his wife, Kathleen, they present a popular workshop entitled, *Self Publishing: All You Need to Know about Getting—or Not Getting—into the Business.*

About the Artist

*K*athleen Burgoon Okonowicz, a watercolor artist and illustrator, is originally from Greenbelt, Maryland. She studied art in high school and college, and began focusing on realism and detail more recently under Geraldine McKeown. She enjoys taking things of the past and preserving them in her paintings.

Her first full-color, limited-edition print, *Special Places*, features the stately stairway that was the "special place" of the characters in Ed's love story, *Stairway over the Brandywine*.

A graduate of Salisbury State University, Kathleen earned her master's degree in professional writing from Towson State University. She is currently Publications Marketing Manager at the International Reading Association in Newark, Delaware.

The couple resides in Fair Hill, Maryland.

**For information on other titles by Ed Okonowicz,
see pages 99 - 106.**

The Original

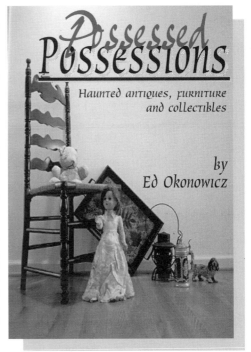

Possessed
Possessions

Haunted antiques, furniture and collectibles

by
Ed Okonowicz

A bump. A thud. Mysterious movement. Unexplained happenings. Caused by what? Venture beyond the Delmarva Peninsula and discover the answer.
Experience 20 eerie, true tales, plus one horrifying fictional story, about items from across the country that, apparently, have taken on an independent **spirit** of their own–for they refuse to give up the ghost.

From Maine to Florida, from Pennsylvania to Wisconsin . . . haunted heirlooms exist among us . . . everywhere.

Read about them in **Possessed Possessions**, *the book some antique dealers definitely do not want you to buy.*

112 pages
5 1/2 x 8 1/2 inches
softcover
ISBN 0-9643244-5-8

$9.95

"If this collection doesn't give you a chill, check your pulse, you might be dead."
—Leslie R. McNair
The Review, University of Delaware

"This expert storyteller can even make a vanishing hitchhiker story fresh and startling. Highly Recommended!"
—Chris Woodyard
Invisible Ink: Books on Ghosts & Hauntings

" 'Scary' Ed Okonowicz . . . the master of written fear— at least on the Delmarva Peninsula . . . has done it again."
—Wilmington News Journal

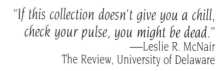

Storytelling World
Honor Award

"[Welcome Inn is] . . . a sort of auto-club guide to ghosts, spirits and the unexplainable."
—Theresa Humphrey
Associated Press

Delaware Press Association
First Place Award

See order form on page 106.

$\mathcal{S}$pirits
$\mathcal{B}$etween the $\mathcal{B}$ays
Series

True
Ghost Stories
from the
master storyteller

Ed Okonowicz

This chilling series, invites you into a haunted house built upon ghostly tales of the Mid Atlantic region.

Wander through the rooms, hallways, and dark corners of this eerie series.

Creep deeper and deeper into terror, until you run *Down the Stairs and Out the Door* in the last volume of our 13-book *Spirits* series.

Volume by volume our haunted house grows. Enter at your own risk!

Coming
next:
Vol. VII
"Up the
Back
Stairway"

A
DelMarVa
Murder
Mystery

*" . . . this is Okonowicz's
best book so far."*
—The Star Democrat,
Easton, Maryland

*" [FIRED!] . . . produces an
interesting glimpse into
the high powered world of
politics with
kidnapping and murder
added for spice."*
—Cecil Whig,
Elkton, Maryland

*"DelMarVa—
a dream state.
Pleasant for some; a
nightmare for others!"*
—Tish Murzyn,
Atlantic Books,
Dover, Delaware

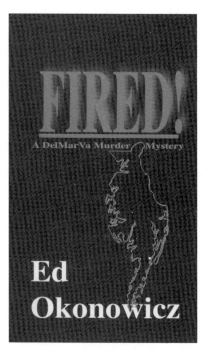

" . . . an entertaining, if gory, murder mystery."
—The Aegis,
Harford County, Maryland

*" . . . full of action, mystery, intrigue and
excitement. To call it a page turner
would be an understatement."*
—Linda Cutler Smith,
Mystery Group Coordinator,
Borders Books,
Wilmington, Delaware

Get FIRED!

*I*t's early in the 21st century and DelMarVa, the newest state in the union is making headlines. There is full employment. Its residents pay no taxes. The crime rate is falling. And, with five casino-entertainment centers and a major theme park under construction, it's soon to be one of the country's top tourist destinations.

Just about everything is going right.

But, in the first year of this bold experiment in regional government, a serial kidnapper strikes . . . and the victims are a steadily growing number of DelMarVa residents.

Will the person the newspapers have dubbed "The Snatcher" ruin DelMarVa's utopian state? Or will the kidnapper be caught and swing from a noose at the end of a very stiff rope—since both hanging and the whipping post have been reinstated to eliminate crime on the peninsula.

In this first DelMarVa Murder Mystery, meet Governor Henry McDevitt, Police Commissioner Michael Pentak and state psychologist Dr. Stephanie Litera, as they pursue the peninsula's most horrifying kidnapper since the days of Patty Cannon.

320 pages
4 1/4 x 6 3/4 inches
softcover
ISBN 1-890690-01-5

$9.95

The DelMarVa Murder Mystery series continues
as Governor Henry McDevitt and his colleagues
solve another mystery in **Halloween House**.
Coming in the Spring of 1999.

"For most of us, Disappearing Delmarva *is as close as we'll ever get to rubbing elbows with real treasure."*

—Brandywine Valley Weekly

Disappearing Delmarva introduces you to more than 70 people on the peninsula whose professions are endangered. Their work, words and wisdom are captured in the 208 pages of this hardbound volume, which features more than 60 photographs.

Along the back roads and back creeks of Delaware, Maryland and Virginia—in such hamlets as Felton and Blackbird in Delaware, Taylors Island and North East in Maryland, and Chincoteague and Sanford in Virginia—these colorful residents still work at the trades that have been passed down to them by grandparents and elders.

These people never made the news; they made America.

208 pp
8 1/2" x 11"
Hardcover
ISBN 1-890690-00-7

$38.00

Disappearing Delmarva

Portraits of the Peninsula People

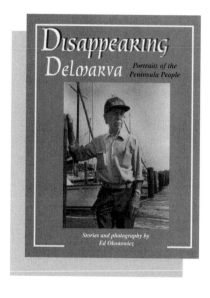

**Photography and Stories
by Ed Okonowicz**

THE BUTLER, THE BAKER, THE
FISHNET MAKER . . . ONCE
FLOURISHING OCCUPATIONS ON
THE DELMARVA PENINSULA . . .
ARE A SAMPLING OF THE MANY
SKILLS FALLING VICTIM TO TIME.

Winner of 2 First-Place Awards:

Best general book
Best photojournalism entry
National Federation of Press Women, Inc. 1998

Complete your collection...

or to be a part of the next book, complete the form below:

Name _____

Address _____

City _____ State _____ Zip Code _____

Phone Numbers (_____) _____ (_____) _____
                  Day   Evening

_____ I would like to be placed on the mailing list to receive the free
Spirits Speaks newsletter and information on future volumes.

_____ I have an experience I would like to share. Please call me.
(Each person who sends in a submission will be contacted. If your
story is used, you will receive a free copy of the volume in which
your experience appears.)

I would like to order the following books:

Quantity	Title	Price	Total
	Pulling Back the Curtain, Vol. I	$8.95	
	Opening the Door, Vol. II	$8.95	
	Welcome Inn, Vol. III	$8.95	
	In the Vestibule, Vol. IV	$9.95	
	Presence in the Parlor, Vol. V	$9.95	
	Crying in the Kitchen, Vol VI	$9.95	
	Possessed Possessions	$9.95	
	FIRED! A DelMarVa Murder Mystery	$9.95	
	Disappearing Delmarva	$38.00	
	Stairway over the Brandywine	$5.00	
	Possessed Possessions 2	$9.95	

*MD residents add 5% sales tax.

Please include $1.50 postage for first book,
and 50 cents for each additional book.

Subtotal _____
Tax* _____
Shipping _____
Total _____

All books are signed by the author. If you would like the book(s)
personalized, please specify to whom.

Mail to: Ed Okonowicz
                 1386 Fair Hill Lane
                 Elkton, MD 21921

Make checks payable to: Myst and Lace Publishers, Inc.